D0435996

SHAME
AND
WONDER

SHAME
AND
WONDER

ESSAYS

DAVID SEARCY

RANDOM HOUSE

NEW YORK

Published in the United States by Random House,
an imprint and division of
Penguin Random House LLC, New York.

RANDOM HOUSE and the HOUSE colophon are registered
trademarks of Penguin Random House LLC.

The following essays have been previously published:
"Hudson River School" in *Granta;* "El Camino Dolorosa,"
"Mad Science," and "Still Life Painting"
in *The Paris Review.*

LIBRARY OF CONGRESS CATALOGING-IN-PUBLICATION DATA
Searcy, David.
[Essays. Selections]
Shame and wonder: essays / David Searcy.
pages cm
ISBN 978-0-8129-9394-3
eBook ISBN 978-0-8129-9395-0
I. Title.
PS3569.E176A6 2016
814'.54—dc23
2014046233

Printed in the United States of America on acid-free paper

randomhousebooks.com

2 4 6 8 9 7 5 3 1

All photographs copyright © David Searcy

FIRST EDITION

Book design by Barbara M. Bachman

For Nancy

CONTENTS

———

SHAME
AND
WONDER

THE
HUDSON RIVER SCHOOL

———

'M IN THE DENTAL HYGIENIST'S CHAIR AND SHE'S A NEW ONE, although very much the same bright, cheery presence as the last, which works for me. The unencumbered heart is best, I think, in matters such as these. She seems about the age of my daughters, which I mention, and we talk. She's from West Texas, where her father is a rancher. I'm a writer. Well, her sister is a writer. Really. Children's books. How about that. It's a nice day. You can see downtown from here. We're on the eighth floor. I've been coming here for years, and I have always liked the view. I think there may be something classically romantic (if that's not a contradiction) about the view and my condition as I view it. Like those grand romantic nineteenth-century landscapes so majestic you don't see at first the tiny human figure there, oblivious and engaged in tiny purposes of his own right at the edge of where the whole world seems to fall away toward heaven. This is just like that except it's Dallas, Texas, with no place to fall away to and I'm only here for a cleaning.

When I'm able to speak again, it is to lie about my flossing habits and ask about her childhood on the ranch—I spent some time on a ranch myself when I was young, pretending to help with shearing sheep and hunting the wild dogs that would prey on them. It's coyotes in West Texas, though, she says. And so develops out of all this bright and cheery and obligatory chit-chat in the eighth-floor dentist's office such a strange, opaque, and mysterious tale, it startles me and makes me ask if she'd mind if I spoke with her father about the events.

It seems there occurred, a number of years ago on her father's ranch, an alarming rise in coyote depredations among his flock. The lambs, especially, suffered terribly. He believed it was the work of a single animal but his efforts to hunt it down were unsuccessful. For two seasons he tried all the usual snares and calls but nothing worked. The animal was too cunning. And the lambs continued to die. One day he hit upon a new idea—and here's the part I'd like to know a little more about and why I'd like to give him a call, find out where the idea came from, whether he made the tape recording for this purpose or already had it; how it felt to do what he did, if it seemed desperate or dishonorable or too risky in some indefinable way—but anyway, one morning he took a tape recording of his infant daughter's cries (not those of Lila, my hygienist, but another daughter's cries) out into the tall grass or the bush, the range, whatever you call it out there where the coyotes wait to take away your lambs, and played the recording as he watched with his rifle ready. And it worked. The coyote came, he shot it dead, the depredations stopped and that was that. She writes her father's name and number on the appointment card and says she's sure he wouldn't mind at all if I gave him a call and that she'll see me in six months.

Six months later I've not called him. Though I've thought about it often enough. I've even gone online to look up Sterling City, Texas—which is the nearest town to the ranch—and used that Google Maps capability that is still, to me, so ghostly, where you're able to descend from heavenly cartographic altitudes right down into the street-level world to pass among the living. I'll pass west on Fourth Street—Highway 87—through the middle of town, which isn't much, proceeding in those spooky-smeary increments of fifty yards or so. You don't just jerk along between the discrete locations like you'd think. They've introduced a bit of theater here, I guess. So when you click from one point to another along the virtual yellow stripe—from here in front of this boarded-up feed store, say, to where that little white-haired lady waits to cross the street on up the block—it all goes blurry, sweeps away to the rear like smoke in a wind before things rematerialize around the next coordinate where you find you've overshot the white-haired lady, have to spin that magic compass thing to turn around and get a closer look. She seems uncertain. She looks past you down the highway to the west, where the town itself blurs away into mesquite and scrub and rolling empty distances. On down the road I pause and spin the compass thing again, but I can't see her. I suppose she got across. I have no reason to believe the ranch is out this way at all. I get a sense of how it looks, though. And it all looks like it's pretty much the same. This sort of scrubby empty country. Line of hills off in the distance. I keep thinking I might spot some sheep or something—maybe a coyote even. Everything's so open. But the resolution isn't very good. Those smudges out there could be anything. A mile or two outside of town the virtual yellow stripe splits off to the left down Highway 158. I drift that way for a while until the sameness seems to settle in completely. Then I stop and look around. I can't tell which is the way to go and for a second I'm like Cary Grant in *North by Northwest,* stuck out here in my business suit in the middle of nowhere, absolutely lost.

I think the view across the city on a nice day from the eighth-floor examination room is better than a fish tank. Although possibly to similar effect. So, here I'm back again and haven't called her father. Lila, I say, I'm afraid I haven't called your father. And perhaps she's disappointed, having told him I might do so. I apologize, explaining how terrifically tangled up I've managed to get in my current project but I really had the time and should have called. There's something here that makes me hesitate.

Back home I open my little kit and throw the floss away, replace my orange toothbrush with a green one. Later on I'm paused on Highway 87 at the edge of Sterling City once again for no particular reason, gazing past the brown brick church and the service station out to where it fades to open country. It's a nice day here, as well. The blue sky hazes into white near the horizon. It's late morning, I would guess. My girlfriend, Nancy, a painter who pays close attention to the way things look and lived in California where they know what coyotes look like, says she saw one near my house once. Right out here in these densely ordinary 1950s neighborhoods one foggy night, quite late. It stood in the grass beneath the power lines that run beside the tollway. She had come across the Northaven bridge and there it was, just standing there long-legged in the grass, in the foggy pale pink tollway light. She stopped and rolled her window down for a better look. And for a moment it looked back, then loped away.

A number of years ago on Forest Lane, not half a mile from here in heavy afternoon traffic, I encountered a giant snapping turtle attempting to cross the road. And it had almost made it somehow, crossing all six lanes but found itself unable to mount the curb. I parked my car to block the traffic, got behind it trying to keep away from the bloody but still dangerous-looking beak—it might have been injured by a car or just from bashing against the curb—but, anyway, this thing was as big around as a trash-can lid and weighed about fifty pounds, so it was all I could do to hoist it over the curb and get it headed toward a narrow grassy corridor that ran behind some houses. There was no place in the area I could think of that might call to such a creature. No place anywhere nearby for it to have come from. But next morning it was gone. I've seen raccoons at night dart in and out of storm sewers on my street. And once, alerted by the yelps and exclamations of my neighbor who was fighting to control her dog, a toad the size of a mixing bowl right out there in the gentle summer evening beneath the streetlamp. I encouraged it—one sort of stomps and lunges—out of the street into another neighbor's yard. Then we retreated—she with her wild-eyed dog and I with my thoughts. That toad was even bigger than the giant African bullfrogs I had seen at the Dallas Zoo. It had no business here. Nor anywhere we care about, where limits are imposed and children sleep and dream unburdened by outrageous possibilities. In the morning though, of course, it too was gone. Where in the world do these things come from? Is the city like a net? Does our imagination—urban, gridlike—drag behind us deeper than we know? And these are just the ones we see. Or are they simply passing through. Unsure of us. Our world perhaps a little ghostly to them, streets and houses hardly here at all, a blur like smoke across an older landscape.

I can't find the appointment card with Lila's father's name and number on it. Which, I imagine, lets me off the hook for a while. But then, a day or two later, there it is, tucked into my wallet. "Lila King, RDH" on the front, and on the back, across a gauzy reproduction of three vaguely Postimpressionistic apples, "Courtney King" and two phone numbers, cell and home. So I call him. What the hell.

He's on the highway in his pickup truck—a good old honest

pickup truck, I'll bet. And he remembers being told that I might call. I can't quite tell, at first, how this is going to go. I like his voice. That broad and easy, pure West Texas way of speaking that I've come to think is somehow fundamental, undistorted, like the structure of a crystal that's had adequate room to form. If I attempt to imitate it—try to demonstrate and let myself get into that West Texas sort of talk, which is the way all Texans probably ought to talk and maybe did before the cities pinched our noses and our vowels—I find it hard to stop. I find I want to be the one who speaks like that, regards the world that way. Whatever way that is. He seems okay with this. Amused a little, maybe. We'll just drive on down the highway—is it 87, I will wonder later—and he'll tell me how it happened, how the whole thing really happened over a long period of time, a generation, in fact, between his tape-recording of his infant daughter's cries and rediscovering them and taking them out there with him to higher ground—a "mountain," as he calls it— maybe sixty miles away where he would spend the night and "come down from on top" at the crack of dawn. That's how he says it. He decided he would "come down from on top."

I'm checking my notes and they don't tell me why it was sixty miles—I'll have to ask him later. Maybe they lived away from the ranch then, or the coyote had been spotted somewhere else, but anyway this draws the process out somehow. Reveals, it seems to me, more clearly something about the strangeness of it. Traveling such a distance with that tape recording, taking it so far away. The boom box—or, who knows, I guess it could have been an older reel-to-reel; I'll have to ask about that, too—but I imagine it beside him in the pickup truck that evening, and this daughter, this same one, Joellen, seventeen now, out on a date that night, I think he said. I think he said the way it happened, she was waiting for her date and he had come across this tape a little earlier and his wife said, "Why not use it? Why not use that tape and see if it comes to that?" As if, somehow, their daughter waiting there so beautifully, I'm sure, and maybe vulnerably as well, brought this to mind. This possibility. And he's heading away that evening, taking all that with him there on the seat beside him (I shouldn't give my imagination so much room, I know. Details are bound to shift.), but there beside him, surely, something to consider as pertaining to the squalling, fragile origins of things. Not to discuss to himself or anything like that but there beside him nonetheless. A hunter's mind, a rancher's mind, you'd think, would have to have a certain peripheral vision, as it were—and maybe that is what you hear in those long, slow, inflected vowels between the consonants like wind between the fence posts, that provisional sense of things not quite in view. Okay, too much. But still— how many lambs had died? He said two "crops." Two years— two crops. All lost, I guess. I hate to think how many fleecy, squalling lambs two crops might be. My uncle Jack, who oversaw that ranch near Glen Rose where I spent time in my teens, ascribed to sheep a strangely maladaptive fatalism whereby, merely nipped by the predator, barely marked, not really harmed at all, they'd drift into a kind of shock or resignation, fail to eat, and finally die. My uncle Jack was more a hunter and outdoorsman, not a rancher. So who knows. Another thing I need to ask about. But I remember one time having to kill a lamb or kid we found near death—a little mark where he'd been bitten on his hind leg. That was all. It makes the wild dog or the coyote or the wolf a kind of metaphor to sheep. It's the approach that counts. The fact of it. The terrible apparition.

In "The Mioritza," the ancient Romanian ballad, a shepherd is told, one night by one of his sheep whose name is Mioritza, that his brothers plan to kill him in the morning and divide his flock between them. Yet the shepherd doesn't flee. He's like the lamb who knows from the touch of death that death is inescapable. So he says to Mioritza—and there seem to be a number of versions, shorter and longer; sometimes, I've been told, the poem, depending on who's singing, may go on and on all night—but fundamentally what he says is: do not tell of my death, but rather tell how I have gone away and married a queen, the Bride of the World; that at my wedding stars descended; that my crown was borne by the sun and the moon; great mountains were my priests, the trees my witnesses, and all to the songs of a thousand birds and the burning of the countless stars, my torches. And thereafter, Mioritza tells this story again and again as she goes wandering over the countryside, across the rivers and mountains to encompass and define, as some suggest, the form and spirit of Romania—and I think this is the part that can go on and on all night.

So Lila's father spends the night up there on the mountain with the tape-recorded cries and, in the morning, "at the crack of dawn," comes down and sets it up. He turns it on low and lets it play for about three minutes, and this is what interests me the most. How was the light? Was it one of those hazy dawns with redness spreading all along the edge of things but not yet casting shadows so it's hard to pick out movement in the distance? Did it take him back to mornings when they'd hear the baby squalling, have to get up in the chill and attend to her, never dreaming this would happen—that those cries might drift away like this, uncomforted across the empty landscape? That's the worst thing that could happen. And yet here he is. He turns it up a notch. And then, not thirty seconds later out of the lifting gloom, the coyote making for him at a dead run. Does he comprehend the risk? What if he misses? There's no end to it then. The lambs will die. The cries go on and on. But at a hundred yards he drops him. Pow. One shot from a .280 Remington with a seven-power scope. The world continues and he pays Joellen the two hundred dollars he promised. She and the next year's lambs grow up. And there you have it. Here again. It was an old one, he says. A smart one. You could tell by the old snare scars. But not very big—maybe thirty-five pounds—which he thought odd. He has the skull and the hide at home.

I hate to floss. It seems sort of prissy—like a manicure or something. But I know I really should. My girlfriend flosses all the time. I can't see Lila's father flossing, though. A toothpick, sure. But flossing? I don't know. How we attend ourselves seems touchy, somehow, out here in the open. Out on the range, the scrub, the prairie or whatever, where a sharp peripheral eye is so important. One's attention should be outwardly directed. I remember on Nantucket once we visited the seventeenth-century Jethro Coffin House. The oldest house on the island, I believe. It's near the center of town but up a little rise surrounded by trees, so it's not hard to imagine the isolation back when it was new. It's one of those massive-chimneyed, tiny-windowed postmedieval houses so protective, so much more concerned with warmth than light, you sense a certain built-in trepidation. There's a clear, mown yard around it and a chain across the open door with a sign announcing times for tours. It's like the houses children draw. It's like the first house in the world. An upstairs bedroom with a cradle by a window breaks your heart. A reluctant window in the heavy white-painted planking of the wall above the ancient hooded cradle with a corner of its little quilt turned back. The bed next to it is completely made, its antique quilt pulled up, a single pillow placed on top. We know they're gone, these people, centuries ago. It's just that cradle's little quilt turned back, receptive still as if to make us think the child is here somewhere, that maybe there's a chance she's not quite lost, that someone yet might bring her, stand there by the window in the evening for a moment holding all that's close and dear while gazing out upon what must have seemed, in 1680-something in the New World, such a terrifying gulf. And for a moment simply standing there, the child presented to it. What has this to do with flossing, you may ask. Well something, surely.

Now that I'm into it I should call him again. To let him know I'm serious. That I've had to put the project aside for a while and now there's time. So it's been—what? Almost a year. And I should let him know I'd like to come and visit. Nancy too. She'd love to come. He seemed okay with that before. It's taken this long just to start and then to figure out which way it's going to go. I ring him up. And once again there seems to be a little hesitation at first but then it's very easy, very friendly—sure, he'd love for us to come. They have a couple of extra rooms and no, the last motel in Sterling City closed four years ago. But we should come. He'll take me varmint hunting, take down that .280, which he hasn't fired since back there on that hillside on that morning. We should come to see the wildflowers, too. They're everywhere. There's been a lot of rain and now they're everywhere and not just bluebonnets either—he can get a little tired of the bluebonnets—but other kinds as well, the Indian paintbrush and the others, lots of red and pink and yellow. It's spectacular right now.

———

I DON'T GET BACK to him till February, though. Somehow. A year again almost. Or I guess I did call once but it was very brief and he was busy; grandkids coming. And by then I'd got all caught up in the novel once more, trying to find the end and taking longer than I'd hoped—an unproductive trip abroad took time, and more time to reveal itself as altogether useless. It's a thing I seem to do—write past, way past sometimes, the proper endings of things. I hope that's not what's happening here. It's hard to tell, though, when you're not so sure what you're up to in the first place. At the very least I'd like to get some photographs of him. Joellen, too, if she's around. And of the coyote skull, of course. The countryside. And the location where it happened.

Anyway, it's February and I see I've got a dental checkup scheduled for the end of the month and figure maybe now is the time to call. That's crazy, isn't it. All this time. But who knows. Maybe there's a process here or something. I'll say, "Lila, spoke to your dad again," and that will take the conversation out into the emptiness, the edge of the world, the prairie where I'd rather be in any case. I catch him puttering around in the garage. It's cold. They've had a little snow. There is an echo to his voice but otherwise it's just the same. A little slow at first. I tell him, Bet you thought you had escaped. But no, that's fine. He's glad to talk. And so we do—about all sorts of things. How I'd like Nancy to do a sketch of the skull if that's okay. Of course it is. He has the hide as well. The pelt. Whatever you call it. A red-tinged one. Your bounty used to get docked for that, he says. Red-tinged, red-tinted. They prefer the lighter-colored ones. The red ones come from the east. It makes good collar fur for jackets, though there's not much market anymore. I like the thought of red-tinged coyotes drifting down from the east, through cities even, ordinary neighborhoods, as silent as the butterflies that come through in the fall. I'm thinking next month, if the weather's nice, might be a good time to come. He thinks so too. And stay in San Angelo maybe, just to keep things flexible. That's not too far. But anyway I'll call.

It's getting close to my appointment so I guess it's time to floss. So I can say, Oh every now and then. Not regularly. But now and then. You know. I've got this implement. A sort of toothbrush handle with the earnest ergonomics of a target pistol grip and at whose working end is a little plastic bow strung with about an inch of floss. These little bow-and-floss assemblies are disposable and subtle and ingenious, with the floss acquiring tension as the bow snaps into a complicated socket so configured as to provide a perfect lockup as the limbs of the bow compress with normal use, but to release when they are pressed against a surface. It has counterintuitive angles. Asymmetrical rubber inserts. It's as if designed by NASA to anticipate all difficulties, all extremes of temperature and atmosphere. Uncertainty, indifference. I have had it awhile and tried it once or twice. And I imagine even lying there unused it must have prophylactic properties. And yet I do not love it. I regard it with suspicion and regret. It's unbecoming, I've decided. So, what makes it unbecoming? Do you think the little birds that clean the teeth of crocodiles are unbecoming? No, of course not. I'm okay with little birds.

The elevator in my dentist's office building has a glass wall that invites you to appreciate the view on your way up. For the first few floors, you're shown the parking garage, but five and above you're looking over buildings, trees, and neighborhoods and then clear out to the skyline—unobstructed here, the whole expanse of downtown, east to west, though in the morning haze it flattens into blurry gray like mountains. Lila's hair has changed from bright and cheery blond to serious brown. I think the seriousness is natural. She spent two weeks, I believe she said, as a volunteer in Africa providing dental services. A pot of boiling water for sterilization. She was amazed at all the things she took for granted.

Spoke to your dad again, I tell her. And we talk about West

Texas and the distance and the drive—not bad, she says. Five hours, maybe, if you stop for lunch. She shows me on her phone a couple of photos. One is a pencil sketch her father did of a French bulldog—the kind she's always loved. He has an artistic side that pops out and surprises now and then, she says. The other is an old yearbook photo that she calls his Holly-wood shot. And so it is. That deep-eyed, square-jawed sort of handsome that can seem a little menacing, might fight on Gary Cooper's side or not. This time it's a pretty easy session. All checked out and ready to go before I know it. Not a word about flossing. It's still early. You can see the haze hanging over the city. There's a smoky-looking layer at the horizon. She presents me with a little plastic bag of dental-hygienic odds and ends. When I get home I'll toss the floss and keep the toothbrush Another green one. That's good. I don't care for orange.

It seems that inch or two of snow they got last month was it. They're edging into drought. They've got the red flag warn-ings up, he says. No rain. Just wind. And dry as it can be. And once a fire gets going, there is not a whole lot you can do. But sure, come on. Just give me a call, he says. I'll meet you on the highway. Bring some rain.

We leave the interstate at Cisco and head south on Highway 206—a narrow, uneventful road that feels, to Nancy, like we've touched down from some altitude into the actual world. I imagine it's like Google Maps to her—the way she dozes, wak-ing now and then from smoky, smeary dreams along the virtual yellow stripe to look about. Where are the animals? she won-ders at one point. She means wild animals like deer. It's open country and you'd think there might be something other than cattle to be glimpsed out there among the scrub and scrubby-looking trees. We stop at a Dairy Queen in Cross Plains. I love Dairy Queens. You hardly see them anymore except out in the wilderness. A sort of consolation. You're allowed a chocolate malt—or that elaborate Oreo-cookie-and-ice-cream concoction Nancy likes—because you're out here at the edge of things where love grows thin and dust (or smoke—I'm not sure which) is blowing down the street. A small and bent (and, I can't help but think, combustible-looking) old man walks in on what appears to be a regular errand to receive, across the counter from a girl who calls him Paw Paw, lunch all boxed and ready to go. To take to Mamaw, he announces. Nothing for him. It's Mamaw's lunch. Does he not feel well? Probably not. He stands outside and waits to cross the street. I'm thinking, What if the Google Maps survey vehicle were to drive by at this moment with its panoramic camera? Then he'd probably get caught like that poor white-haired lady. Standing there in the blowing dust with Mamaw's lunch forever. Mamaw waiting. Hope departing in the red-flagged afternoon.

I spent some time in San Angelo once when I was little but I don't remember this part north of Highway 67 where it all goes flat and indistinct. The Chicken Farm Art Center bed-and-breakfast doesn't proclaim itself. No flashing neon rooster in a nightshirt and beret like you'd expect. Rather, it seems to disappear out here, submerge into the natural loss of clarity and category. Just the way things tend to run together as they fade out into prairie, which I think is what you see, or certainly sense, as a kind of emptiness down there at the end of the street. We take it slowly, let the spirit voices guide us.

It's all here, though. Even a restaurant they've installed in an old feed silo. And what must have once been henhouses given over to artists and craftsmen whose products appear to issue forth about as easily and automatically as those of the former residents. There are available rooms. A couple of importuning cats. It's pretty active on the weekends, we are told. But this is

Monday. Not much going on. One studio is open. We peek in. A little girl is taking lessons in mosaic—somewhat incongruously from a painter of dramatic and spontaneous sumi-e horses who seems oblivious to her difficulties. I don't think it's going very well. She stands at a table pushing colorful shards of tile around. Her teacher nods and smiles at us. The pieces are too big. She's got this delicate little diagram—a flower or an animal or something—and the tiles are way too big to make any sense. Perhaps it's sumi-e mosaic, but I don't think so. It's a problem of resolution. In the courtyard there are glass-topped tables here and there opacified by a layer of dust. There's been a lot of dust, our hostess says. We get the Santa Fe Room, a poster of a painting of a pueblo scene confirms. It's from an Arizona gallery Nancy showed in, very briefly, years ago. The cats are out there all night long. Sometimes we hear them at the window.

In the morning the cats have joined me at the table I have dusted off to share my blueberry scone (which is the breakfast part of the bed-and-breakfast deal) and help me wait till nine o'clock, when I've decided I should call. I am reluctant. I think maybe I'm imposing too much on this whole thing. A pretty simple, even delicate sort of thing. But come on out, he says. I scribble down directions. He will meet us at the turnoff.

Nancy loves to travel anywhere. Especially on exploratory missions where you get to take your time and look around. And look around is what there is to do out here. Your eye goes way out to the hazy edge of things. You're like a panoramic camera. The periphery is everything. When she and I first met, I told her stories of how Dallas used to be. How, in the sixties, you could drive north past the edge of it and find yourself in farmland, open country. Now, of course, you can't. The city and the suburbs have expanded and there isn't any north edge anymore, although I told her we might try to find a remnant if she'd like. And so we did. It took an afternoon—like trying to find a childhood scar that's drifted, over the years, across the body. It wasn't much. No more than twenty acres, near some railroad tracks, that seemed to have been under cultivation until recently, or maybe just a haying field—I think there was a tractor under some trees. But we got out and all around you could hear traffic and we thought, Well, this is it, the ancient shoreline where the Greeks made camp outside the walls of Troy, where you could stand and gaze upon the empty world.

We get to the turnoff but we're early. He's not here yet. So we park just off the highway next to the white caliche road that leads dead straight out into nothing as if that were its intention. We get out. It seems like how the world must look when you're not looking. Settled back to fundamentals. Like that Englishman who, awakened in the middle of the night, will have no accent, speaks like anybody else. I find a .270 Winchester cartridge case on the ground and show it to Nancy. Somebody must have spotted a deer, I guess. She holds it to her ear. She is listening to it whistle in the wind. I want a picture of the road before he comes. Before a cloud of dust suggests there's something out there after all. Right now it makes a perfect diagram— converging lines transferable to a warning sign: watch out, this road goes on and on forever. Now he's here. A huge dark pickup truck has pulled in off the highway. Not the way I was expecting. Cloud of dust as he emerges—massive, smiling, cowboy-hatted, gray-goateed, tooled leather suspenders. Later, Nancy will decide he has Roy Rogers eyes. She always loved Roy Rogers and that squinty, soft amusement in his eyes. I'm going to say the English actor Oliver Reed—though Oliver Reed awakened suddenly in the middle of the night because the cows are loose or something and he hasn't time to change into

an Englishman. My hand is gripped, enveloped, and within about a minute I am offered chewing tobacco—which I actually consider for a second as a test I'm likely to fail—and then a nickel-plated, lavishly engraved Colt .44 for our protection. I believe Roy's having fun, but I don't care. It's nice engraving. Not as good as factory, though, he says. It'd be worth more with factory engraving. Here we go. I run to the car to get my hunting knife. A good one, too. Handmade with a nice stag grip. So, see? I'm armed. And rather stylishly, in fact. We follow him out the white caliche road to nowhere. Nancy's laughing. What? Five minutes and you start comparing weapons. She keeps laughing. And they're both such beautiful weapons, dear. Shut up, I try to explain. No, you shut up. No, *you* shut up.

It's a large and handsome limestone house on top of a hill. I think it might be the one we noticed from the highway coming out, way in the distance. Who lives there, we thought. I'm sure we thought. What must that life be like? And now we're there. We're here. A little brown dog named Scout is running around and trying to make its yapping heard above the wind. The wind is steady. As it ought to be, I guess. There's nothing out here to discourage or inflect it. You can see the distant hazy edge of everything from here. And then so strangely way out there to the north and west and barely emergent from the haze (I think they use a haze-gray paint), as if belonging to those fundamental properties of things you never see except when things reduce like this to fundamentals, are the giant wind turbines, the really huge ones with the football-field-long blades. So that's where wind comes from, you'd think if you didn't know. Of course, it has to come from somewhere.

Everything up here on top of the hill is new. They built the house about four years ago. The heavy, limestone-founded, iron-railed fence. And, so precariously it seems, on a lower terrace on the west side near the fence where the hill drops suddenly away, a beautiful playground for the grandkids. Tent-roofed structures—we would have called them forts—on stilts with slides descending, one a giant twisty yellow plastic tube. Suspended tire. Rope-ladder rigging. And a swing set with three swings, each plastic seat a different color—not-yet-faded yellow, blue, and red. A choice. And then which way to face: the house across the drive just up the hill or that great emptiness toward which the hill drops off right there, not twenty feet away. To which you'd sense yourself presented every time at the top of the arc, where letting go—to a child especially, I imagine—always seems a possibility. In the big high-ceilinged living room are all the animals Nancy didn't see on the way down. All the ones she'd periodically wake herself to look for out in the scrub along the highway. Here they are. The biggest elk I've ever seen above the fireplace. On the floor, a brown bear rug. And on the wall across the room above the bookcase is a group of horned and antlered beasts so fully and expansively themselves they lose significance as trophies. They are specimens. All "fair chase," though, I'm told. "I wouldn't use a blind. That's bullshit." And the meat, where appropriate, consumed. So they are cleanly, self-sufficiently here. The animal representatives. And here and there among them, family photographs. A needlepoint genealogy. I think the newness throws me just a bit. He says his family has been ranching for a hundred years out here. And yet it's like they've just arrived. Or maybe just arrived again. To build a house like this, a big receptive house like this out here, must be a different sort of undertaking. Not like in the city, where the concept is established, no particular risk involved. Out here you probably need to know a lot more clearly what you're doing. How to situate yourself. You've got your basics here to deal with after all. Your wind, your emptiness, your animals, your house. He stands in the middle of the living room and looks wherever I look, seems to reappreciate these things. One photograph I return to is a black and white of Courtney and his brother from the fifties, each boy posed identically dressed in cowboy hat, fleece-collared jacket, jeans, and boots behind his fat prizewinning sheep. It looks like Courtney wears his older brother's jeans, the cuffs rolled up. It's perfect somehow, in that fragile-yet-momentous way that some Walker Evans photographs are perfect. Courtney's brother—you can't quite make out, so must infer, his freckles—grins at something off to the right beyond the field of view. While Courtney and his sheep—their faces calm and close together at the center of the picture as he hugs her about the neck to hold her still—gaze out at us. They make an emblem against the dead white-painted clapboard barn behind. I take a picture of the picture. Of the elk. The other creatures on the walls. A massive grizzly skull he shows me. And at some point—I had hoped to wait for this, I think, to put it off, to try to settle back into what I imagined I was doing here—he's standing there holding the coyote skull. So small in all of this. A tiny thing. Like something lost and found—Oh, here it is. He holds it out. He holds it very lightly like it's glass. I hear the women in the kitchen. Lila's mom, Elaine, looks very much like Lila. In a group of Walker Evans faces, she would be the pretty one. The wind is really kicking up out there. I take a picture of him standing there like that. And then a close-up. And he has the hide too, right? He does. He brings it out. The whole thing—dangly legs and tail and everything. The superficial coyote. Like a ghost. Where are the scars, I ask. He shows me on the legs the smooth black marks left by the snares. I ask Elaine to come outside on the porch and hold it for a picture. In the wind it flaps like paper. Like it wants to blow away.

In the early nineties when this happened they lived north of here, in Snyder, where the girls attended school. The ranch— a lease—was sixty miles away, near Silver in Coke County. Coyotes, Courtney tells me, almost always come in about the first of September. Yearlings usually, driven from other ranges. Most of these are taken with snares. This one was older. He had females with him, too. A male will generally hunt with a female. They shot three of his companions. But each year he'd have another. After the second year he'd killed about 120 lambs. A three-pound lamb can get to ninety pounds in three and a half to four months if the range conditions are right. Sometimes a coyote waits. If there are rabbits to eat—and in those years there were; a "surfeit," Courtney says—a coyote will wait until a lamb weighs maybe twenty pounds. A lamb, of course, is easier and fatter than a rabbit but, somehow, he knows to wait. How strange to think about a coyote out there—what could be more simply, purely present than a coyote—a coyote out there thinking of the future as if it were just a simple thing like dust or wind or something. Nancy's sketching in the kitchen. There's good light in there. She's chatting with Elaine. The coyote skull is on the table. Courtney's brought out the .280 that he hasn't shot since then. Except for the buttstock, it's entirely camo-taped. He says he did that while he waited on that morning. Not so easy, I imagine, in the dark. We're in the living room. He's got his tools to reattach the scope, to put the rifle back together as it was. He says that third year, about the third week in April after they had gotten through with shearing, there was a perfectly calm and moonlit night so he drove to where the sheep were gathered, parked and spread his bedroll out in the back of the pickup truck, lay down and waited. It was midnight probably, maybe a little later, when he heard the coyote howling. It was very still and the howling was right there,

"like right up on you." Then the sheep began to run and bleat and he raised up with his rifle in the moonlight—but no coyote. He had taken what he wanted. After that they pulled the lambs off the ewes and put them in the feedlot to protect them and that worked pretty well for the lambs but then the coyote went for the ewes.

Andrew Delbanco, in *The Puritan Ordeal,* attempts to understand the Puritans' sense of evil in the New World. How it changed. How, in the emptiness they found here, it condensed out of that vapor they'd imagined as the absence—the "privation"—of the good into a thing, an actual presence. It's as if in such uncertainty, such emptiness, they needed more than anything to situate themselves securely opposite the danger. Had to sacrifice a bit of hope for that and place themselves, a little more deliberately, in the world. I like to imagine the Jethro Coffin house brand-new. On that hill above Nantucket a couple of generations after what seems to have been a sort of spiritual discouragement. Its newness still expressive of the general arrival, I should think. The tiny trepidatious windows peeking out upon the dark. Late in the book Delbanco quotes the Romanian religious historian Mircea Eliade, who notes that "any village anywhere *is* the 'Center of the World.'" And, by extension, any house.

I ask Elaine at one point, "Doesn't it get lonely?" "No," she answers almost before I get the question out. It doesn't. It gets late, though. Light comes in at a softer angle. Afternoon is wearing on and I've not asked to see the tape. I'm not really sure I want to hear it. All the tapes are kept together in the top drawer of a dresser in the guest room. All the predator-calling tapes. I hadn't realized. But certainly that makes sense. Why should you have to be a musician, as it were, with horns and squeakers or whatever—though he uses those, as well. Why not just get a recording of what you want. And what you want is very specific forms of misery. I look through them: "Chicken Hen Squalls," "Gray Fox Distress," "Young Turkey Distress," "Mad Crows," "Raccoon Fight," "Baby Crying (Joellen)." Really. There with the mad crows and the others. These things happen after all. These small misfortunes. Raccoons fight and babies cry. It's touching, though—the parenthetical attribution. Almost reluctant. He knows very well he's placed her in that range of possibilities. That the coyote doesn't care—he's looking way beyond the personal. So it's not "Joellen Crying." That would not be parallel. But still—as if to say I know, I know. He's got the player, too. Not the one he used back then but one just like it. Dusty, scuffed black box like evidence recovered from a crash site. In the kitchen Nancy's finishing a sketch, a nice one on gray paper. Simple side view of the coyote skull in charcoal with white highlights. Courtney takes a seat and places the recorder on the table. "Want to hear it?" He leans back. He has a toothpick in his mouth. See? What did I tell you. There's no flossing. There are no flossing habits here. But here? I'm thinking. Should we really play it here? Right here in the kitchen? In the fading afternoon? Elaine is standing. No expression. "Sure," says Nancy. What is there about the toothpick? As he gazes down. The thoughtlessness. Or no, it isn't thoughtlessness. My God. It's like a shock. I sort of expected a little accidental background noise or something, a little preparatory blankness. But it's right there. Fully present. Six weeks old, I think they said. A shriek to take your breath away. The way a baby shrieks to end all shrieks—all shrieks contained therein, all forms of misery, the wilderness itself. Elaine has backed away. Of course the coyote came. How could it not? It's all right there. And it goes on and on. I'm looking at Elaine. Okay. She hears her baby out there in the wilderness, I'm thinking. But it's not quite that. He

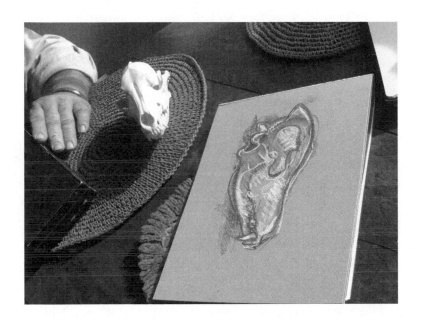

shuts it off and looks at her. "Oh my," says Nancy. "What?" he says. Or maybe I say, "What?" Elaine says, "Why didn't you pick her up?" Oh my. She's gone right past the coyote and all that. Back to the baby at that moment. "Why did you let her cry?" "I didn't." Courtney smiles. "She wouldn't stop." She knows, of course. They know all that. So I just go ahead and ask the thing I want to ask, insert the big idea where it won't fit, I'm pretty sure, where it seems awkward and impractical—and Courtney's so polite, they're both so kind to let us come in here like this so he just listens to me, smiley-eyed, as I get all jacked up to make him see what must have been there in his heart, the faint suspicion on that morning on that hillside as he played that tape that something more was going on. He had to sense it, right? That there was something more at risk. You know. Perhaps there were misgivings. Sure, he knows. "Hell no," he says. "I wanted to kill it."

———

THERE HAS BEEN, along with the drought, the wind, and the constant threat of fire, another hovering concern. Just after Christmas, a young girl disappeared not far from here in Colorado City. Courtney's eleven-year-old granddaughter lives near there. It was believed at first that the girl, thirteen, had run away from home. But pretty soon it began to look like an abduction. Attention turned to the mom and her live-in boyfriend. There were reports of child pornography and drugs. Failed polygraph tests. I'm not even sure in what connection this came up in conversation. We were talking—Courtney and I; Elaine and Nancy had gone off by themselves somewhere—about the coyote and the tape. About that ranch they had back then—and which I wish it had been possible to visit and is out that way, just down the road from Colorado City. It was on his mind. On everybody's mind, I guess. The miles between these little towns seem so completely empty, like a vacuum, no resistance to events, so when a fire pops up or someone disappears, it's like it's right here, right outside. So people talk about the danger, what to watch for. There are certain things he told me. Not just things like don't get into cars with strangers. But more subtle things. For example, if you hear the water running after dark, don't go outside; they'll cut your water line to make you come outside. Or if you hear a baby crying. They will do that, too. The very same thing. To bring a woman out. A girl. "They will go out to that," he said. Can you imagine? What if you heard that crying out there in the dark? Not even thinking of the danger—just the emptiness of that. In every sense. No parenthetical attribution there, for sure. No hope at all. Do not go out. That child is lost. Like running water. Irretrievable. Like the wind and smoke and threat of fire and everything. You can't do any good.

———

AFTER HE KILLED IT, Courtney waited about a week then went out calling to make sure. Just to see what might turn up. I should have asked what kind of call he used—I'm sure he's got all kinds. He could have used a blade of grass for all I know. Back then before the drought they probably had some grass. That's what my friend across the street would show me how to use when we were kids. His father was a hunter and he showed me how to take a blade of grass and sort of stretch it out between your thumbs and blow. It made a reed and sounded awful. That's a rabbit when it's hurt, he said. And I remember wondering—I was probably eight or nine—why in the world would you want to make a sound like that? But anyway, he's out there calling—out in the bush, the range, whatever; out where the coyotes wait and listen—and he's out there quite a while but nothing comes. Until, at last, a little gray fox shows up—this sounds like a fable but it's not. This little gray fox comes skidding up within five feet or so. Starts barking at him. Barks and barks. And this is good, thinks Courtney. Coyotes tend to kill or run the foxes off. So this is good. No coyotes. Just this little gray fox that keeps on barking at him. Courtney grabs a handful of dust and throws it at him. Fox just backs away and keeps on barking. I didn't know a fox could bark. But this one does and won't go away. And as he tells me I keep seeing this, imagining it, as if from a certain distance. From a certain elevation as from a prominence somewhere, with Courtney standing way out there in the middle of nowhere and this little gray fox just barking. From this distance, very faintly. Barking and barking. And that puff of dust dispersing in the wind.

EL CAMINO DOLOROSO

I HAVE THIS STORY FROM THE ARTIST TRACY HICKS ABOUT HIS former father-in-law, who had a 1960s pickup he'd restored and customized—spent years on the project, loved this truck like nothing else—until one day he backed it over one of his kittens in the driveway. Killed the kitten. Sold the pickup truck. Like that. Well, that sort of sums it up, I thought. That pretty much says it all, it seemed to me at the time. Is metaphor everywhere? Of course it is. Once consciousness, once meaning gets a start it keeps on going. You get literacy and metaphor and God.

The thing about custom cars and hot rods—glancing through a copy of *Rod & Custom* magazine, you can see they tend to grade into each other—is the strangely counterintuitive sort of dreaminess involved. I haven't checked to see if angel hair is still the concours style but it was when I was a kid. That ectoplasmic spun-glass stuff they'd use sometimes in school plays to suggest a mist or heavenly atmospherics. You would see these cars at shows—again, in magazines; I never went to a show but I was fascinated—and they'd always have these cloudy mounds of angel hair around them. Underneath and around the tires, like they were floating. Not entirely of this world. And yet so massively mechanical and sculptural. The custom cars especially, which, although they'd generally have these gorgeously chromed and souped-up engines, seemed intended more as presence, pure idea. And the idea, I think, was more or less that paradise is possible. That you can actually get there in the proper frame of mind—which those archetypal chopped and purple-painted '49 Mercurys sought to represent. They'd hover just above the ground—no more than a couple of inches' clearance, I would guess—sustained by angel hair, it seemed, and not much else, the wheels a concession, a politeness, ornamental and vestigial. I remember thinking how extraordinarily cool that looked. And how impractical. How could you drive that down an ordinary road? The road would have to be like a showroom floor. Where would you find a perfect road like that? Like in a dream. Where would it lead? Yet here were the means for such a journey—as gloriously real and here-and-now as they could be. Which was the point. That they were not like concept cars, those empty visions of the future that manufacturers like to roll out on occasion. These were ordinary cars transformed. Revealed, in a way, as what they ought to be. And were, essentially, we were allowed to feel. The marvelous implicit in the everyday. How striking and encouraging to discover that a '51 Ford pickup or whatever had a soul. Who would have thought? So, get behind the wheel of that and where do you go? Can you imagine?

Tracy's father-in-law, it seems, had had a pretty rough time in the war. He'd been in the infantry, in the thick of it. He'd tramped all over Italy, Tracy says, came home dispirited and worn out, wanted safety and a wife and a little frame house in Marshall, Texas. All of which, by the time we're talking about, had settled into a fairly grim, habitual sort of life. His teenage bride had borne two daughters very early, lost her youth, and

grown into a disagreeable, sharp-tongued woman Tracy remembers in the kitchen mostly, cooking and complaining at
her husband, who was forbidden to smoke in the house and so
would sit outside the kitchen in the carport smoking and talking to the cats. He had a morning-to-early-afternoon job at the
railyard running a huge machine that straightened railcars
damaged in collisions and derailings. It was quite a thing to witness, apparently—how this machine could grab a twisted box-
car, pick the whole thing up and bend it back into shape. You
tend to think of travel by rail as pretty safe: it's all laid out, after
all; you can't get lost; there's nowhere to go but where you're
going, but maybe not. Among the people who would come by
now and then to watch him run the operation was an auto mechanic friend whose personal project was a wrecked but restor-
able El Camino pickup truck. Well, this guy seems to have died
and Tracy's father-in-law was able to buy the pickup truck and
take the project on himself. It wasn't all that old. Not like some
classic you could excuse yourself for spending too much money
on. I'm sure he could have bought an unwrecked used one for
far less than he eventually would spend. But you know how,
when something's wrecked, you kind of see it from a distance,
see right past it toward what could have been and might be
yet if you just take your time, don't try to rush it. In such circumstances one can glimpse perfection. So it was with Tracy's
father-in-law, I guess. This truck became a thing of beauty.
Not a full-blown "chopped and channeled" concours queen, of
course, but given what was possible back then in Marshall,
Texas, pretty nice. And better and better all the time. A fancy
paint job—two-tone metal-flake gold and cream. Gold rolled-
and-pleated leather seats with matching visors. Lots of little
things, as well, to keep him busy afternoons and on the weekends in the carport with the cats. He'd get it washed and

checked out weekly. Once a month, he'd change the oil. Sometimes, says Tracy, he'd just sit there in the carport with it. Cat in
his lap, just sitting there and smoking and, I have to imagine,
season after season, soft habitual sounds of cooking and complaining from the kitchen contrapuntal to the purring in his
lap, just gazing off across the sadly less-than-prosperous little
neighborhood and down the little street to God knows where,
to who knows what subliminal paradise, not knowing really,
consciously, I'm sure, but still, you'd think the heart must seek
a destination.

It was early one winter morning when he backed it over the
kitten. Tracy heard he never drove the truck again and very
quickly it was gone. And so, within a couple of years, was he—
from cancer. Not much time to sit with nothing under the carport. But I bet that's what he did. Just let the air come through
and sit out there and smoke. What would you do? You couldn't
move. How could you not just sit there and blink your eyes at
having it all break down like that, a bump in the road—not even
a bump; you hardly feel it, but you know. That's it, you think.
Right off the rails. Can you believe it? Just like that. You have
to wonder what to retain of a thing like that. Do you remember how it was? And maybe hold it in your thoughts? Or let it
go and learn your lesson. How you can't get there from here.
How love obliterates itself. How you should probably just keep
still for a while and let the other things come back. The other
cats, the less beloved ones. Their little water bowls and dishes
here and there. The early morning sounds of movement in the
kitchen.

MAD SCIENCE

———

THINK I NEED TO FIGURE OUT WHAT I WAS DOING, WHAT I really felt I was up to, as a kid when, overwhelmed by some enthusiasm, some new all-consuming fascination, I'd require it to be fully expressed at once. I'd have to slap together something out of household odds and ends, available parts, to represent whatever it was, to come to terms as quickly and flimsily as possible. And generally leave it at that. And here I mean only the usual sorts of things you would expect to have engaged a dorky child's imagination in the fifties—shortwave radio, rocket ships and outer space, the more spectacular forms of science—and, in the better class of dorky child, to have engendered actual seeking after knowledge, the discovery of the glory of the thing in its machinery.

I knew kids like that. And admired them all the more to the extent I failed to appreciate that what they really loved was the machinery, the procedures toward a practical understanding. Strength of character, I preferred to believe, explained it. How they'd suffered through the tedious fundamentals to receive, as an award it seemed to me, the apparatus I so envied. That the visible instrumentation might be secondary, merely

an extension, an uncelebrated consequence of studious application to the principles, not sought, nor forced, nor longed for
in itself but rather simply coming to be there all around you in
your bedroom easy as anything, as naturally as toys or sports
equipment, unselfconsciously as that, was a dismaying possibility. It made me wonder sometimes if those kids, smart as
they were, knew what they'd done, what they'd achieved, what
all those dials and lights and switches, curly wires and metal
rocket parts and laboratory glassware really meant in the overall view of things. One's distant and incapable view of things.
Which I may actually have felt permitted insight and perspec-
tive unavailable to the competent and concentrated gaze. I may
have felt I'd caught a revelatory glimpse of something way out
there, the glint of all that stuff, the shimmery sense of it, so
delicate, thin as paper—cardboard maybe, which is generally
what would come to hand when I would try to model it, in-
voke it with some taped-together cargo-cult construction on
my desk. It could be anything. The look was what you wanted.
The gesture. The idea of dials and switches seemed enough.
So, what idea? Enough for what?

What, for example, was I thinking turning my mom's old
record player into a seismograph? I mean, my goodness, 78 rpm.
That's good for what? For Guy Lombardo. Smart cocktails and
fleeting moments. Not the slow, eternal creaking of the earth.
You've seen a seismograph, of course, the clocklike turning of
the chart against the stylus. It's a meditative instrument. It listens. It has nothing to do with 78 rpm. And I knew that, I really
did. Yet here I had this thing all set up with a coffee can or
something wrapped in graph paper and a brick on top to keep
it on the turntable, coat hanger bent around and straining to
present a stub of pencil to the chart, and a wire—just plain utility wire—that led from the coat hanger all the way across the

room and out a window to a steel rod I had shoved into the ground. And just that crumbly black clay ground that we have here in Texas. The kind of ground that grounds things out, where hope and energy go to die, that's not much fun to play in, even. Hard to dig. What information did I think might come from there? What was I thinking? I had read enough to know you needed bedrock. Who had bedrock? Maybe those smart kids. Not me, though. No bedrock here. No fundamentals. Yet it wasn't an altogether empty gesture. It was hard to let it go.

Once you'd assembled your imaginary instrument, you needed an imaginary quantity, imaginary causes, fainter and fainter suppositions strung together in a Zeno's paradoxical sort of way on out the window to converge upon the vanishing expectation. Say there were out there in the yard—in everyone's yard, the common ground—unlikely properties, effects oblique and subtle and evasive to which bedrock, proper seismographs, and smart kids were insensitive. What if there were vibrations of so high and fine a frequency (the properties of Silly Putty, recently discovered, came to mind) that dirt might act more like a solid or a gel and send its pulse through slack utility wire like wind through weather stripping, mournful saxophones at New Year's. I don't actually remember turning it on. It would have tugged against the weight, the brick and everything on top, to get to speed. And then the coffee can would not have been quite centered, so the pencil would have skipped and dragged and skipped and dragged like time to change the record. And I bet it was a nice day, too. A weekend probably, kids outside, one's whole life out there waiting as I'm standing there, watching this little mark get darker and darker on the pale blue-gridded paper, as if meaning might accumulate or something.

Hank Van Wagoner was the most spectacular smart kid in

the neighborhood. And though a few years older than the rest of us, he counted still, I felt, as an impossible example to my superficial longings. He lived two or three houses down and we could hear him testing rockets in his backyard sometimes, usually on weekends. Bear in mind that this was before those little foolproof rocket kits came on the market in response to general horror at the mounting number of injuries sustained by young enthusiasts. The call to space rang clear across the land, and none of us who chose to answer was discouraged in the slightest. It was easy for a kid to buy explosives at the drugstore, bring a bag of potassium nitrate home like jelly beans. Though Hank, of course, had progressed beyond such simple solid fuels into the truly touchy realm of liquid propellants, which included caustic, toxic, self-igniting "hypergolics" such as hydrazine and something called "red fuming nitric acid." So we listened, in our own backyards, my parents in their folding canvas lawn chairs, with some interest.

I remember a test so loud it woke me up one Saturday morning, sent me running down the alley. I have no idea where Hank's parents were. I hardly ever saw them, don't recall his mom at all. His sister—rumored to be, in her own way, as precocious as her brother—was an intermittent, dark, alluring presence in the evenings on the balcony outside her little suite above the garage. In any case, Hank seemed to suffer under no constraints and here he was, while other kids were rising to Rice Krispies and cartoons, about to blow it all to hell. A rocket engine, when it's working most efficiently, is pretty close to blowing up. You *feel* it. You don't have to know a thing to sense some limit is about to be exceeded. It's ecstatic in that way— you grip the Cyclone fence, your face against the wire. You note how close he's standing to it. Is he crazy? There's no smoke, just hard blue flame and a roar like nothing you're prepared for in the general calm of 1957 or '58, when leaves were raked and airplanes still, for the most part, had propellers. How can he have a thing like that? How can he stand there like he knows what he is doing? It's suspended from a sort of parallelogram that's hinged, I see, to swing up with the thrust, which is recorded by a marker on a graduated chart. All this is clear to me as small details are said to be at the moment of one's death. This sort of noise can only mean that something terrible is happening, or we've passed beyond the normal intuition. Surely everyone can hear it. Surely all the other kids can hear it, paused before their TVs, their Rice Krispies suddenly silent in the bowl. And then the flame is yellow, sputtering, and the parallelogram goes slack, rectangular again. The other noises of the neighborhood return—I can't recall but I imagine barking dogs and screen doors slapping. He had stuff you can't imagine—some sort of rocket-tracking radar thing he showed me once, my God the dials and switches. And a ten- or twelve-foot framework— maybe six inches in diameter, longitudinal spars and bulkheads made of welded steel and weighing probably fifty pounds—he gave me. The absurdly overbuilt interior structure of some liquid-fueled experiment. Some rocket never launched, I think. Sure, take it. And I did. I dragged it home and leaned it up against the fence, amazed, bewildered like a member of some preindustrial tribe deciding how it might be hammered into spearpoints. There was nothing to be done with it. My longings seemed to get all tangled up in the rusty pragmatism of it. Here was fundamental structure, to be sure. The wind blew through it. Had we honeysuckle growing on the fence, it would have made a sort of trellis.

Here's what I would do: I'd pack an aluminum tube with a fifty-fifty mixture of potassium nitrate and sugar—wooden dowel jammed in at one end and a Testors model airplane enamel screw cap with a quarter-inch hole surrounded by a bunch of little holes because it looked cool at the other—glue three cardboard fins and a cardboard nose cone on, apply the paint (all-over silver with red fin tips), touch it off, and watch it melt. What was I thinking? And I mean it. What was this half-assed demonstration all about? I knew you couldn't make a proper rocket nozzle out of a screw cap. I could have told you it would blow right out, that the glue and the cardboard fins would ignite. The melting—more like wilting—aluminum tube surprised me, though. You see, we do learn from our failures.

Have you ever seen Olivier's film of *Henry V*? How carefully it graduates reality from act to act, unfolds it like a pop-up book from stage and painted scenery to something close to real although compressed into the conventions and teetery perspectives of the fifteenth-century miniature. And holds it there. You wait for another jump. For the origamic sets to fall away and the play to charge straight out into the world. And it almost does. The massive chivalry of France comes pretty close to bashing through—you think the churning, swampy earth can't get more real than that but then the battle's over and you look around and find that the rolling distances enclosing all this realistic mayhem are imaginary still. "What is this castle call'd that stands hard by?" A miniaturist, imaginary castle folded into painted hills. It's Agincourt. You think of Krishna's admonition that the battle is a dream—and how, you want to ask, how is it, then, one's duty to do battle is not also an illusion? And why is the inconsistency so thrilling? So ecstatic to imagine that we merely represent ourselves. That our going through the motions might be everything.

Sometimes, on Saturday mornings when there wasn't something noisier going on, you'd hear a kid named Lefty coming up the street. That wasn't his real name, which was Gilbert, nor even descriptive, I don't think. I guess it was just a name he liked. You could always hear him coming up the street because he always kicked a can. And it was always pretty early. I imagine the opening eyes of sleeping parents. Here he'd come. Way down at the end of the block you'd hear him turn the corner. And remember, cans were heavier then. When kicked, they went much farther and produced a clearer note. I felt it counted as a sort of public service. Rise and shine. But bright and early as he was, he was benighted. Seventeen years old, I think he told us once. And very tall. But acting, seeming, more like six. We didn't quite know what to make of him. He'd pass by Saturday mornings—pass right through us in a way, past even our instincts to make fun—and that was usually all we'd see of him that week. One thing about him we admired, though, was his sidearm. It was a Hubley Colt .45 in a leather holster. And although, at eleven or twelve, we no longer placed toy guns at the top of our list, you had to respect the Hubley Colt .45. It was the fanciest, most expensive cap gun out there. No one else had one—a full-sized replica of an 1860 Colt with a brass-plated cylinder that functioned and received six realistic-looking bullets, each to be realistically charged with a single cap. You had more firepower, I suppose, with one of the ordinary types that loaded endless rolls of caps. But that was different. There was no conviction there. No sense of the almost real about it. Someone loved him. Someone had said, Here, Gilbert. Here for you is something very precious, just like you, and almost real.

One Saturday morning Bobo Riefler and I were standing in my driveway and waiting for Lefty. In the garage I'd put together a sort of laboratory: anything that looked good from my chemistry set; a big glass vat (I'm not sure where that came from) full of water into which had been dissolved whatever chemicals were left in those little square bottles, plus a sprinkling of potassium permanganate—wonderfully explosive when mixed with glycerin (just the one-ounce jar please, thank you, and a pack of Dubble Bubble), here though merely for the vivid, toxic purple—and right next to which I'd set up one of those "traveling arc" devices with its brilliantly ascending and expanding, zapping discharge so beloved of mad scientists and which, I had been shown by one of the smart kids, could be made from a discarded neon sign transformer (half-burned-out ones still were capable of 15,000 volts, produced a two- to three-inch spark, and could be had quite inexpensively); and, finally, gathering all this up in a philosophical sort of way, attached imprecisely here and there like ivy, coils of wire meant to conduct by faith alone the whole idea, whatever it was, the very spirit of mad science, to a leather football helmet I'd suspended over a borrowed canvas lawn chair.

I would like to suggest that Lefty was our choice for reasons other than unkind ones. Though we were unkind of course—so, as for that, I'm pretty sure what I was thinking. Yet within that there was something else, I want to say: surprising, not unkind. I don't remember what I told him. But I don't think it was difficult to get him to come with me down the crunchy gravel drive to the garage—a little two-car frame garage, quite dark, not finished out or anything, just studs and planking, garden tools and stacks of cardboard boxes, all the stuff that tends to wind up in garages, with my laboratory over in the corner and the lawn chair by itself out in the middle of the concrete floor. I think what was surprising was how easily and heavily he sat there. How resigned he seemed to be. His six-gun shining—those holsters alone cost a fortune. So, I'm standing at the switch—and naturally nothing's going to happen; nothing ever really happens. But you never know, it's God's domain, and here it's such a beautiful Saturday morning, all our lives aglow out there, somehow, and glaring through the single open over-head door into the dark garage. And Bobo's finally sort of calmed down, thinking who knows what but waiting. And then after I throw the switch we're all still waiting there for a second or two, all three of us, the zapping of the traveling arc behind us, gazing out into the glare as if some limit were about to be exceeded.

A FUTURISTIC
WRITING DESK

———

THE RELIGIOUS AND THE MODERNIST IMPULSE SEEM TO SPRING ·
from the same engulfing moment of self-consciousness and
doubt. "My God, where are we?," then a space of ten or twenty
thousand years to give us time to wander out into the shallows,
gathering shells and stuff exactly like we're not supposed to
do, before the secondary wave brings in the terrible apprehension once again. It seems so hard to know what we are really
doing—what it all comes down to, finally. I remember an exhibition of modernist objects at the Dallas Museum of Art a
number of years ago—for the most part just the commonest
sorts of things we're used to living with, but emerged from this
terrific redesign, this reappraisal toward first principles as if, to
our surprise, such thoughtless accidental things could have first
principles or even be adjusted to suggest the possibility. Is this
what we've been doing all this time, it made one think, when
we thought we were only sitting down or making tea or listening to the radio? Is this what we've been doing? How extraordinary, beautiful, uncomfortable and strange our lives have been.
And maybe risky too, somehow. The very idea that there might
be a pure idea about such things appears to force, or reveal, a

certain instability. The eye, the hand attempt the thoughtless move toward such a thing as they have always done and then you think, Well, have I got this right? Am I positioned in the way I ought to be?

Nancy and I once took a trip to Enchanted Rock near Fredericksburg, Texas, to try to escape some personal anxieties of mine. I was not happy. Things had not been going well on a variety of fronts. So off we went in that uncertainty to climb the great peculiar four-hundred-foot-high hemispherical, spalling granite bulging-up of forces deeper than can easily be made sense of. I was her bearer, carrying giant rolls of drawing paper big as sails that caught the wind and needed little boulders brought to hold them down and sometimes needed me to hold the boulders as she drew. If you've not been there, it's a pretty spooky place. As if mitosis on a planetary scale had been arrested at some point in the Precambrian to leave this half-emergent, asteroidal sort of world as a place where one might actually stand upon first principles and try to keep one's balance. Not so easy, as it turns out. So coherent and extensive a distortion takes you with it. Halfway up you've lost your proper sense of ground and start to feel the near horizon as the clearer one, the granite one toward which a simpler Yves Tanguy–like flatness falls away. There's nothing picturesque—not even scary eighteenth-century picturesque—about it. It subtends the picturesque with an idea that's hard to get across, to keep your footing on. On our way down we found ourselves having to cross great slabs of spalling rock. These are the slabs that, broken and weathered, make huge Yves Tanguy–like shapes upon the Yves Tanguy–like surface—so uneasy, that surrealistic sense of things as simply, purely strange. Depictable strangeness you can point at and describe and even come to regard as familiar, in a way, without depleting its expressiveness of underlying strangeness as an irreducible property. The fact of strange as something to consider along with up and down and near and far and so forth.

We had come to a place where we had to step from one vast, weathered spall of rock to another across a gap of maybe a couple of feet. No more that that. Quite deep but just a step, which I had managed without thinking, rolls of paper on my shoulder, Nancy standing on the other side with her box of art supplies, as I remember, though she thinks it was a backpack and that maybe it was earlier in the day when we were simply scrambling around, exploring. I recall it differently. With evening coming on. Wind picking up. I waited, maybe to take her hand, or not—sometimes it's better not to interfere. And yet I did. I made a joke. A little tease. "Don't fall," I said. A look of mock concern. Or maybe "That's a long way down." Or maybe just the look. And she stepped back from the edge and looked at me and found herself unable. Couldn't do it. In a minute she would force herself—she won't submit to being afraid for long—but in that moment she just stood there, as did I on the other side, unable now, myself, to step across and join her, stunned to be there all of a sudden as if stricken with self-consciousness or something, with the whole thing so unsettled, all my worries and the gravity here so out of perpendicular, the ground itself not altogether clear, not quite developed yet as place distinct from object, and this gap, this gulf between us where the rock was breaking up that I just had to go and point out like an idiot, just at dusk, wind whipping through the rolls of unsuccessful drawings (she would tell me later how she couldn't seem to find the proper edge, the boundary for a drawing; how her eye kept sliding off). As if such gaps, such inconsistencies were not all over the place up here, the funda-mental state of things, in fact—the deep and dangerous give-

and-take of ground and object. But I had to go and point and say, Oh my, look where we are and how precarious this is. And we could hear the other climbers coming down. Faint clumps of voices here and there beyond the limited horizon coming and going with the wind. And way down there at the bottom everything in shadow now—the little stream, the parking lot and visitors' center. How I loved the visitors' center—pamphlets, maps, displays; the crummy telescope you plunked a quarter into for a strained and blurry view as if it were some sort of planetary body you were gazing at, a glimpse of where mankind might one day venture at his peril, with his children on his shoulders, picnic lunches, plastic water bottles, silly-looking hats.

That instability must be built in, I think. That terrible give-and-take. We seem to reenact it all the time. How long did the Buddha take—the Buddha, for God's sake—to complicate into those marvelous polychrome and polybrachiate "deities"? A thousand years or so?

By the time we got down to the bottom, it was nearly dark and deer were everywhere. We'd heard there were too many for some reason—odd climatic circumstances, too few predators. And here they were emerging from the trees, all rather small and probably hungry, coming right up to the path. One sniffed my hand. We spotted thirty or more on the road back into town. The dark was full of them. That night I got a call and had to head back to Dallas in the morning. But before we left that morning, Nancy waiting in the car, I finished off a really terrible bottle of wine from one of the local vineyards—probably a product of the same climatic circumstances. All the grapes of every kind surviving some big hailstorm had gone into it. And it tasted like that, too. Like screw first principles, just get me on the road.

―――

THE AUTISTIC ANIMAL BEHAVIORIST Temple Grandin, through her own unstable sympathies, has shown how cattle, urged along a chute, will balk at an unfamiliar object like a paper cup left carelessly in their path. Get rid of the paper cup and off they go to the killing floor as easy as you please. But just like that they're overwhelmed. A simple, thoughtless little thing like that will bring them to a sudden realization. Stop to notice and you're lost. Sun going down, wind whipping up. My God, where are we? We would really like to turn around and go back to the pasture where we came from but we can't. We must proceed.

I have acquired a list of the objects from the modernist exhibition. (It took some time and a helpful "imaging technologist" in the archives since there was no published catalog.) There is more than I remembered. So much of it, I suppose, I walked right by. It's not like paintings. It's just stuff. It is, in a way, the very idea of all this stuff. Not all of it picked up off the beach, as it were, and cleaned and reappraised to the same degree. There's all this silverware, for example—Contempora salad fork and dinner fork and so on. Century soup spoon. In the little thumbnail photos with the list it's hard to tell what makes them modern, what has happened to them. Not too much, I think. The ornament scoured away in the surf. But maybe back in the thirties there was just the slightest tingle in the hand to pick these up, like accidentally brushing someone's sleeveless arm. The slightest question. It's so strange how things look strange devoid of ornament. How things can get so simplified there's almost nothing there—these points of contact, simple ordinary contact, with the world called into question. Here's a clear glass Corning Silver Streak electric iron from just before the Second World War. It's beautiful. But how does it feel to press your clothes with that? Beyond the visual sense of mass, what else is lost? How clear do we want such things to be? Do we want to lose the heavy moment? Slip away into the future with our chores?

That night in Fredericksburg, we spread the one big drawing Nancy had done out on the bed and found that she had drawn a face. She hadn't realized, but up there in the wind and cold, her paper trying to blow away, her ideas sliding off, her hand had found a face in the rock. A great big rocky face—an ornament. A handhold. Reassurance, I suppose. She'd no idea until we rolled it out and there it was. How about that. That's what ornament is for. To give us purchase. Show how things entail and anchor one another. Spread our understanding out. Extend our grasp. Keep things from being too surprising.

What I mostly tend to remember from the show—my main impression walking through it—are the fragile, simple surfaces of things. A decorative surface ages gracefully and easily. It's already formally compromised and mutable. These surfaces, though, were singular, exposed and unprotected. Taut. Like membranes pulled as tightly around the idea as they could be and, in most cases, showing strain. A little Rudolph Schindler writing desk from the thirties, listed here though not depicted, I remember especially—very small and made of simple painted wood, so tightly folded around itself, some pure idea of itself, so tensely here-and-now, so free of ornament and history, its cracking and abraded surface seemed about to burst, to let it go ahead and slip into the future. With no past, where else to go? I wanted to sit there at that desk, to try imagining the future as a special form of history. Writing letters. Growing old, thin-skinned and startled into the future, onto the killing floor wide-eyed and sitting down. My goodness, such a sad and clear and urgent thing, it seemed to me, that little desk.

I loved the future as a child. Which sounds like a thing a child would say. A peculiar thing to be able to say. The darnedest thing. But that's how I thought of it. As simply as that. Nostalgia, maybe, as a kind of redirectable potential. Personal history nonexistent, what do you do? You think if you hold yourself correctly, get yourself reoriented, you can cast yourself, present yourself, that way. I can remember persuading my mom, somehow, when I was eleven or twelve, to buy me a Danish modern armchair. I'd decided that was it—the very thing to situate me in a clear, anticipatory sort of attitude. To face the future seated and relaxed meant you were ready for it. I cannot imagine how it passed beneath my father's frugal gaze without objection or concern. That he would not have paused at least for a second there outside my bedroom, glancing in to ask himself why should his son possess a Danish modern armchair. And deciding such a question asked too much, I guess. And so it probably did. How to articulate the rigorous imprecision? All the hard, pragmatic thrust and brace smeared out into those curves in such a graceful contradiction that knew how, exactly how, to take the weight without constraining one's position, which, in a Danish modern armchair, was encouraged to be variable, slouched, uncertain, ahistorical and open to all sorts of possibilities. I knew what the future held. There was no question it was airless, black and empty but for rocket ships and blobby-looking stars. But mostly black. That's what you'd see, what you'd imagine from your Danish modern armchair with your homework on your lap, your mom and dad still watching TV in the den—*The Honeymooners'* pointless self-inflicted difficulties, Lucy's crazy struggles and deceptions. You could feel yourself detached, uncomplicated, free to lift your eyes from these impossible problems to the window, to the blackness that, as we know now, is death, the future's only critical feature, the essential apprehension. But back then you weren't so sure. You didn't know so much about it. That it might not really be a place to go.

SEXY GIRLS NEAR DALLAS

—

'VE DECIDED TO LOOK UP CARS ONLINE. I STARTED TO WRITE "computer": "look up cars on the computer." I just barely hear the awkwardness, the old-fashionedness, of that. I've had a computer for only a few years—five or six. My children finally shamed me into it. Anyway, my little Honda has begun to show its age, so here I'm scanning thumbnail images of Volvo station wagons. A bright and virtuous array. You can't go wrong, I tell myself, with a Volvo station wagon. Nothing else provides that same ingenuous, truly voluntary style of practicality—receptive, never submissive, to the burden. For the money, of course, one could go for the sleek and insulated self-assertion of an Audi, say, or a little BMW. Yet one must decline, to choose, in this case, openness and kindness and forgiveness of life's bulkier contingencies, embracing, as an elevated concept, everydayness, life-in-general here at home. To demonstrate to all concerned that you're pretty happy where you are. You've got your red ones, blue ones, silver, black, and white. I like the white. I pause on that one. White looks fine. It's going to be just fine, I think. We tend to think. And then descends across the screen—or simply appears, I can't recall—a little ad. What is the word for when that happens? There's a word. You've got your mind on what you're doing, eyes adjusted to the glow of all the tiny possibilities, and then this thing drops down like a rubber spider on a string. As clear and simple and alarming and imperative as schizophrenic voices probably are. "Go kill John Lennon." "Sacrifice your son to Yahweh." Or whatever. Here in the middle of the easy, cheerful yearbook shots of Volvos, like a whisper, like a leaf onto the surface of a pond, this ad drifts down. "Fuck Sexy Girls Near Dallas." That's it. And below, five little animated photos of the sexy girls themselves. What can it mean? I mean, I *know* what it means but what can it *really* mean? Not "Might I care to . . ." "Please accept our invitation . . ." "Come on out . . ." Somehow beyond mere exhortation of the sort you used to get in the backs of comic books: "Hey, Boys! Have Fun with Chemcraft." Out of nowhere. You will do it or you won't. It makes no difference. There is nothing more to say. Unless you click on it, of course. Which I am not prepared to do.

I am a prude. And there are rules. Rule number one is if you find it—or it finds you, as it were—then it's okay. That's ambient culture. You're allowed to have a look. And maybe even take your time, install your monocle, peruse the publication that's been left there on the cistern in the bathroom of the warehouse where you used to work. That colorful brochure someone has dropped in the post office parking lot may be retrieved, examined for a moment in your car, the sounds of traffic out there, daily life, a buzzing in your ear. Get in, get out is the main thing. Keep your critical distance. Don't go native.

On the other hand, this ad may suddenly vanish on its own. Whatever algorithm sent it here to haunt the bland, complacent

Volvo customer is subtle and may understand the limits, the diminishing returns. The window's open. I'm permitted. It's like standing at the urinal and this is on the wall. You can't just look away. Which brings us to the second rule: You can't just look away.

How sweet and sad they are, of course. How could they not be? They just barely move. As if they weren't quite sure what they should do but here they had this capability built in and why not use it, so each naked sexy girl is told to move a little. How? Well, just a little. You know. Back and forth or something. And they do. The sexy girls sway back and forth. One sexy girl has breasts so large they don't move with her very well. They tend to stay right where they are. Remain at rest. She looks so young to be so anchored—universalized like that. It can't be easy. Are they out there now, I wonder. How near Dallas might they be? Just right outside the city limits like those fireworks stands I used to love to go to with my dad on the Fourth of July? As near as that? That was so wonderful. To head out just at dark, beyond the neighborhoods in those days, past the streetlights into planted and unplanted open regions, to the edge of town and there they were, the corrugated structures with their fronts propped open, bare-bulb-lit explosives of all colors, types, and potencies, degrees of complication glowing softly in the dust of cars departing and arriving. Raking headlights like a prison break. My God, you crossed the line and it all seemed crazy. It was possible to feel that here was everything worth having, every ordinary, slow, drawn-out desire tamped down into combustible units. All those warning labels. Do not hold in hand. Unless that's what you have in mind.

I can't imagine such things now. The ordinary life, the city just go on and on. There is no edge of town. Or maybe south there is—beyond the city limits there's a gradual end to things out Highway 45 toward nowhere in particular. There are empty stretches that way. Certain places where you might pull off the road at night and roll your windows down and turn your engine off and wait.

DIDELPHIS NUNCIUS

MY DOG ROCKY—"OUR GANG" COMEDY–LOOKING PIT BULL
mutt—is an idiot but he's good at catching possums. Or he was
before his hind leg gave out. Even now, though, every couple of
months I'll go out on the backyard deck in the morning, bend
to dispense his pint-mug measure of Science Diet, note his
slow and strangely patient panting, and become aware of another off to the side as gray and weathered as the pressure-
treated lumber, tongue hanging out, little Xs for eyes. Where
do they come from? Why do they pass this way at all? They do
not learn. Or it doesn't matter. In his prime he might get two or
three a week—not counting all those little pink ones tossed like
seeds from nursing females. I have one of those, from June 2005
the label says, curled up in a little jar of alcohol. They're shadows till he grabs them. Then they're real for a second or two.
Then shadows again.

When I moved here with my daughters, ten and twelve, my
teenage son, and a couple of floppy, friendly dogs oblivious to
possums, it was hard. For the girls especially. So uneasy. Families break up for such subtle, imperceptible sorts of reasons. My
wife, Jean—dark, pretty, thoughtful, sad, and distant—always

said we live too long. We're not designed to just keep going. We're supposed to get run over by a mastodon or something long before the conversation starts to slip. One day I picked them up from school and brought them home to a different house. You can't explain it. You place flowers in their rooms—the girls' rooms down a narrow hall at the very back of one of those early fifties houses built out here on the postwar grid as life returned, spread out, and settled onto the surface where the cotton used to grow. And you still sense it. Forty or fifty years later, you're still able to feel that thin necessity. The sudden, somehow incomplete transition. How the simple, low-roofed, rectilinear neighborhoods retain an almost agricultural feeling of exposure and fragility. The flowers weren't much help. Nor my suggestion, quite sincere, that neighborhoods like these provide perhaps the last clear manifestation of the colonizing spirit—and, besides, we had a shopping center they could ride their bikes to. And I used to hang out here myself, had friends who lived out here when I was in high school. I can show you where they lived and tell you stories, cannot stop myself no matter how you roll your eyes and wish things could return to the way they were. Our lives had sort of sifted out, or had been sectioned, cut across at a certain level and exposed to the air. And everything was sensitive, reluctant to be touched.

So maybe that first night I'd tell them bedtime stories like I used to. They'd make fun but what the hell. That's what you need out on the prairie, on your own beneath the empty sky. It's what comes naturally, after all—the endless, animal-populated tales of deep, uncertain meaning. Even John, at seventeen, could be amused. The girls—Elizabeth, the older one, and Anna—would object, think me too jolly for the circumstances. Yet I would persist. They seemed so isolated down there at their own end of the house. In their peninsular little bedrooms looking out through curtainless windows into the backyard, toward the alley where the unfamiliarity lay dark and undisturbed. You can't just say good night. Well, here we are at the edge of the known world. Off you go. Sweet dreams. You need a story. You need deep, uncertain meanings—rabbit, fox, and bear to come and act them out, to hover over like a mist above the cotton fields. Or maybe Mr. Possum. Than whom, I'm convinced, there is no deeper, more uncertain animal.

You know how things get sectioned for analysis. It's how you see what's really going on inside a specimen, of course. A tissue sample, meteorite, whatever: slice it, magnify it, and the operating structures come to light. It is destructive but it works, reducing everything to level, common terms. It pulls the curtain back. Oh, Lizzy. Such a lonely little room back there. I know. And Anna's too, but especially yours. It broke my heart. All by yourself down there at the end where you could see straight out across the dark backyard, across the fences and the other dark backyards, the cold, eternal, light-years-distant gleam of backyard security lights. But here's exactly where the operating structures are revealed (I think at that point more to my delight than yours). Exactly how things are discovered that you didn't know were there.

Had I begun to tell a story? Had I been to John's room first, then Anna's, sat by each a moment, done my best and been dismissed? It's only Dad. It's what he does—makes light of everything. Well, everything is light now, isn't it, Lizzy? "No," you'd say and shake your head. And I'd bend closer, imitating Homer Simpson imitating wisdom: "Isn't it, Lizzy? Isn't it?" "No." Had I begun to tell the tale? "Once there was something . . ." I don't know. I can't remember. I remember how the shadows on the wall became the story. Something moved. Once there was something like the shadow of a possum. Then it moved. Well, look at that. We never had a magic lantern show before. Look how he creeps along the shadow of the fence. He's out there somewhere, isn't he, Lizzy? And we're looking back and forth between the shadow and the window but there's nothing to be seen directly out there in the dark except the backyard lights, of which the nearest seems to cast the shadow. I go over to the window, kneel to bring my eye to intercept the line between the shadow of the possum and the light. It's one of those mercury-vapor lights, I think. That cold, discouraging light that hardly ever needs replacement, burns forever behind the garage and in the interstitial regions where one hardly ever goes. I move my head a little, side to side, to try to find the possum. There's the fence line. Where's the possum? He should be right there. His shadow hasn't moved. I move a little, keep the light above the fence. There. Now he's moving. It's an astronomical moment. There. The mercury-vapor light dims, brightens, dims. It is a complex occultation. He's an inference like those extrasolar planets they detect by noting subtle, regular dimmings of their stars. One cannot know these things directly. One requires the proper instrument. The mediating principle.

Did you know astronomers actually used to ride inside the two-hundred-inch Hale telescope on Mount Palomar? And maybe they still do from time to time, although I doubt it. I imagine it's all remotely monitored now. But they used to. They would ride all night up there at the top in the "prime focus cage"—a cylindrical room they fit behind the secondary mirrors at the point, eighty feet or so above the floor, where all the light from the primary mirror came to its first and purest, widest-field and deepest-gazing convergence. There were other, smaller mirrors—complex sequences, in fact—that they could introduce to redirect the light wherever they wished, including, down at the end of a billiards-trick-shot series of reflections, into the temperature-stable coudé room, where permanently stationed spectrographs received it. These reflections, though, involved a certain magnifying strain and degradation of the image—whereas "riding the cage" meant cutting right to the front, where, for the first time, the observer stared like Perseus straight down into the pristine first-reflected light. It's hard to imagine. It was probably the final, highest expression of stupendousness in science. The mechanical, intuitable extension of our longings. Russell Porter, the artist and engineer who helped design the telescope and established pretty much inaccessible standards for the cutaway illustration, drew a series of remarkable extrapolations from the blueprints. One shows someone (one of the project engineers, named W. D. Burton, it is thought) at the controls of the "prime focus pedestal" in the center of the cage. He's hunched above it, peering down into a tiny guiding eyepiece as he grips one of a system of handwheels used to keep the photographic plate on target. He would have hunched like that for hours at a time as light accumulated gradually on the plate—though probably not in suit and tie as shown. He is idealized somewhat, like his surroundings. As if he, too, were extrapolated. Drawn with that same angular yet modulated clarity, his surfaces described, articulated—shine of combed-back thinning hair, meticulous wrinkling of his suit—as if he had been engineered along with the rest of it. It's touching to see it formalized like this. The everyday inserted here, the suit and tie and shiny shoes and wire-rimmed spectacles as part of it. Placed up there at prime focus like it belongs at the edge of everything. What would he have been looking at? Not much. The cold, discouraging gleam of the guide star in the cross-hairs. Not much more than that, I think.

———

THE OTHER DAY I asked Elizabeth if she remembered how it felt, back there in that little room at night. Those first few nights before we got the curtains up. Did Mr. Possum come around much? Was it hard to get to sleep? I imagined she would have stayed awake and looked for him—his shadow on the wall. Or, actually, walls. Somehow her room was a sort of panoramic camera, other backyard lights and windows figuring into it. I think maybe I remember one time peeking in to see him turn the corner. It all lined up exactly right to show what it was possible to know. Once there was something. But she didn't stay awake, she says. And so the possums vanished until Rocky came along a few years later.

I would love to be able to do a Porter drawing of Elizabeth back then in her room at night. My artist girlfriend, Nancy, might be able to pull it off. She did a wonderful Krazy Kat cartoon for me that's dead-on. Here is Burton, I'd explain, as imagined in the prime focus cage suspended at the top of the largest telescope in the world. Make it look like that. See if you can get that subtle, hazy, silvery, dreamlike glow to everything. The cool, fastidious surfaces. The loneliness. The sense of loss and wonder. Have her sitting up in bed and turned to face the wall behind her. Porter liked to draw these delicate white lines with tiny arrows to define the beam and angle of the light and its reflections. That might work. Between the window and the shadow. Have the room be nearly empty. And be careful with the shadow—her attention is the focus, not the shadow.

And perhaps a little extrapolation here might be in order. A little stupendousness, as silly as that sounds. (A little traveling music, Jackie Gleason used to say.) Imagine a great hemispherical dome like Palomar but bigger. Maybe something like that immense and strangely futuristic cenotaph for Isaac Newton that Étienne-Louis Boullée proposed at the end of the eighteenth century in a series of almost hallucinatory renderings. How fearfully, somehow, it seems to emerge in its own planetary shadow, its own night, into a ragged revolutionary dawn. You want Enlightenment? Well, here. It's not exactly what you thought. The monumental ambiguity. But anyway, like that. As big as that. And the interior very much the same as well—completely spherical and empty. Though in this case with a great horizontal slot cut through to the sky for about one-quarter of the circumference at an elevation thirty degrees or so above the equatorial level where a mezzanine directly below the slot provides an observation floor. Stay with me here. The dome itself, like Lizzy's room, becomes the instrument. The mediating principle. The slot, the backyard fence. And here's where Porter's style comes in—it's mostly atmosphere. It's all inside the empty dome. Gauzy, silvery air and simple, vastly curving surfaces. Some people on the mezzanine for scale—so small you can't tell what they're wearing. Maybe lab coats. Togas. Ordinary dress. They're lost up there. Above and behind them you can see the night sky wheeling past the slot. The endless stars. Can you imagine the quality of dark in there? Imagine how you might not want to whisper lest your soul escape into it. And yet Porter plausibly dilates how we see it. As if starlight were enough. No white lines here; just the faintest indication, slightest brightening of the starlight-brightened air, a brighter dark, comes through the slot, expands and plays against the far side, where perhaps a third—a huge rectangular section—of the spherical interior seems to present a darker surface, like a blackboard, to receive it. This is a photosensitive surface that, on clear nights, can be activated, forced to stay awake all night, night after night, for years or even centuries.

Stupendousness requires that possibility. To give the informa-tion time to gather—random starlight, faint, discouraging, light-years-distant fact of starlight to accumulate around some sort of shadow of the deepest, most uncertain understanding. Not much more than that, but wouldn't that be something, after all.

When we got Rocky he was a puppy, so it took a while be-fore the possums started to appear—or reappear. I'm told they live no more than two to four years in the wild, which is un-usual for a creature of that size. As if they never quite evolved beyond some kind of strict necessity. Some fragile, thin neces-sity. I guess when this was cotton fields or sorghum, pasture, prairie, or whatever, they would have inhabited the strands of forest here and there along the creeks. But now that we're here, so are they. They came along to eat our garbage, get our dogs worked up at night and, if we happen to observe them, reas-sure us inexplicably. Oh look, we sort of start and sort of sigh, it's Mr. Possum. So substantial in his insubstantiality—and yet it all works out. He comes and goes. And even Rocky, dim and hollow as he is—as faintly, gradually as information accumu-lates in him—contains, or represents at least, the understand-ing that there's nothing but the stories that we tell. Good dog. That nothing else helps very much to mitigate our loneliness, our distance from ourselves. And that it doesn't change a thing that, every now and then—say, one in thirty, one in fifty—having hauled another to the alley, laid him carefully in the grass outside the fence, you'll come back later and discover he has gone.

THE DEPTH OF
BASEBALL SADNESS

—

Ignorance

DON'T KNOW ANYTHING ABOUT BASEBALL. I NEVER EVEN
learned the rules beyond the basics of softball I picked up from
watching my daughters play when they were little. In the fifties
it was pretty much assumed, if you were a guy, that you played
baseball, knew the rules, possessed a stack of baseball cards, a
bat and glove—the glove, for me, was the mystery. How to get
that big orange leather glove to fold around your tiny hand
like that, acquire that oily stain of competence that deepened
toward the center where the impact should arrive. That you
and it should be so much of a single mind about this thing.
Even kids with no conspicuous interest or ability would show
up now and then—it must have been a seasonal thing—to hang
around, just hang around, with a glove and a ball to whack into
it as a thing to do as thoughtlessly as chewing gum or puberty
or something. Bobo Riefler, for example, had no special love for
the game as far as I could tell. What Bobo loved was fiddling
with his bicycle, tricking it out with various gizmos of debat-
able utility like those little loops of belt leather he would wrap

around to dangle from the axles to keep them shiny, fastened under with big jewel-like red reflectors. Even so, when it came time, he'd have that glove. As if brought forth from his subconscious fully broken in, attested to by signatures of worthies even I had heard of, black-stamped declarations as to features, style, and general suitability. And his name too, of course, in ballpoint blue along the wrist strap or the side of the pinkie finger, blurring out into the orangey-yellow cowhide like an old tattoo.

I had a glove. I owned one. But had never come to terms, somehow. Whatever those terms were, I had not come to them. Not that I was incapable. I could throw a rock or even—should the occasion require—a spear about as well as anyone. To hurl a rock, your arm gets like a whip. A spear (unweighted stick) goes sideways, though, if you sling it; it requires the forearm snapping to the left as you release. I could outrun the other neighborhood kids except, sometimes, Wayne Flemming. And when leaping from the swing for distance, I knew it was speed not height you needed, how to hit the ground and roll and come up standing. Not go sprawling on my butt. I did just fine with that. But put me out in left field in the morning—God, I hated P.E. first thing in the morning, with that sad, old scratchy morning devotional version of "You'll Never Walk Alone" still in the air, the implication that our circumstances justified such desperate reassurance—and I'd die. I'd be no good. I would be worse than nothing. Measurably. Statistically—say, twice as bad as, possibly even three times worse than nothing. An embarrassment is what I was. Ground ball to left sneaks through on an error: that's one you don't see every day. Boy, that's one for the books; what do you call that? What in the world do you *call* that? Fielder's taken off his glove to get down on his knees and build little houses out of rocks for ants. Did you say ants? The ball sneaks through because he's busy making little houses for the ants? Well that's just crazy. That's just nuts. And so it seemed. And so it was. And why on earth would ants need houses?

My glove came to me on an impulse from my father. I was maybe eight or ten and we were driving back—my mom and dad and I—from Estes Park, Colorado, which he liked to visit in the summer, having worked there on a dude ranch as a young man in the thirties. We'd been driving much of the day in our unair-conditioned Ford through all that featureless expanse of northwest Texas. It was cooling off toward evening and we're getting pretty close, a couple of hours from Dallas, and at that point things seemed quite relaxed and settled into one of those inexplicably perfect moments, of which I recall a few in my life, when all the usual urgencies fall away and there's a kind of neutral buoyancy, a kind of equilibrium or something. Cars still had those little side vents then, ahead of the crank-down windows in the front, and wind came through there pretty well so you could lie down in the backseat and appreciate your passage into cooler air and, after a while, the slight deceleration and deflection of intention from the highway to whatever little town it was and something there of interest we might even stop to visit if it's open. And it was. It was the Nokona factory store, where handmade baseball gloves were sold. And when we came back out I had one and I remember it being dark. Though that does not seem very likely—that a store like that in such a tiny town would keep late hours. I imagine what I've done is let the whole thing slip into a kind of darkness, let the leather-fumigated dark of sleeping with that glove that night wash out across the whole event somehow. Or maybe it was closed but someone still inside to answer a special appeal from my dad, who, though quite stern in many ways, was very good in situations where a point of flexibility was needed. Getting things to work out, finally. I was given to know that this was a special thing but did not constitute a charge, an expectation or a promise to participate—he was busy in those days and very tired when he got home—so more a simple understanding. Well, I guess this is your baseball glove. The kind of understanding you arrive at when things clarify for no particular reason, and the natural forms of things can briefly settle into place.

Formality

WHEN I WAS VERY SMALL, LIKE FIVE AND SIX, I HAD A REGULAR BABYSITTER— portly, cheerful, widowed Mrs. Wilson—at whose home I would be left sometimes when my mom and dad had plans to be out late. She would hide pennies about the house and let me keep whatever I found, then put me to bed in a huge, high, white-bedspreaded bed by a window, open in the summer, facing the street and, just across, a neighborhood baseball field. I knew it was a baseball field. I must have known what baseball was. In any case I'd lie there watching the young men warming up. It seemed so risky, heedless, how they slung the ball around from base to base and even into the dirt as hard as they could to make it difficult, raising little clouds of pink-red dust that hung for a while in the field lights, which had just come on to signify, to me at least, that deepening distinction between regimes— the one where I was in the bed across the street in the gathering dusk and the one emerging on that harsh red dirt, which seemed so uninviting, not at all the sort of dirt a kid would want to play in. Little cars and plastic dinosaurs would not do well out there, it seemed to me. It seemed to me you had to know what you were doing. That was dedicated dirt. There were conditions. What emerged out there so clearly, as the evening closed around it and the people with their lawn chairs and their soda coolers gathered, were conditions altogether unlike those obtaining here on the clean white bedspread by the window in the dark.

So, what is happening in this moment? We've the origins of baseball like a myth. Here's how it started: someone watching from a window on a pleasant summer evening, it emerges. Lights come up. The ground turns red. How much of this is really true?

I've gone back recently. That part of town has not changed much. The field looks pretty much the same. The backstop structure—galvanized posts and chain-link fencing—shows no signs of being any newer than my memory. There's a look old galvanized steel gets as the zinc wash wears away and rust starts showing a depleted and inactive sort of stain, as if the chemistries of air and heat and zinc and steel and memory have neutralized somehow, found some agreement. Mrs. Wilson's house is gone. There's just a vacant lot, which strangely works for me—my ancient witness ghostly, purified, suspended at the height of that big bed above the grass. When I was there a couple of days ago I noticed a policeman parked nearby. And I remembered there had been a terrible incident not far from there a week or so before—a girl discovered behind a dumpster, naked, stabbed, but still alive. I couldn't recall if anyone had been arrested. But I figured I'm too old to be a suspect now. I get to be a ghost here with my notebook, which I hope he sees me writing in, recording faint inscriptions in the concrete made when it was poured, I'm guessing maybe seventy years ago. No trouble here, he must be thinking. Just some harmless old eccentric kneeling, studying the concrete. Taking notes. Which is just crazy. Which is nuts. But surely harmless. What has that to do with anything, I'm sure he thinks. The crap we have to deal with—death and violence, terrible suffering—every day.

I'm able to make out only two names in the concrete—
actually, one name written twice. It's so abraded, and the two-
foot letters spaced so far apart it's hard to see that they make a
name. I stand away a little. "JOE." Big capital letters. And then
off to the left, much smaller, "JOE" again, above a single capital
"G." I'm thinking this one is the first. And seeing how it went
so well, he was encouraged. Got expansive. Put his shoulder
into it. Both hands on the stick. Forget the "G." Just Joe. Not
Shoeless Joe. Not Joltin' Joe. But Joe before all that, as clear
and thoughtless as it's possible to be right here, you see, at the
beginning.

Loss

SEVERAL MONTHS AGO AT A DOWNTOWN BREAKFAST GATHERING OF
friends, I met a young man named Dave England with his wife
and their baby boy. Dave wore a Texas Rangers baseball cap, a
heavy full black beard I vaguely recognized as current bullpen
fashion, and a T-shirt with the image of a cartoon superhero
labeled SABERBOY. I'd later go online to learn that SaberBoy per-
sonified a currently trendy statistical pragmatism known as sa-
bermetrics (from the initials of the Society for American
Baseball Research), a nontraditional approach that had been
celebrated recently in the movie *Moneyball*. But at the time I
sensed only some sort of inside baseball joke and wondered
about it and about what seemed the earnestness, perhaps
the perseverance, underneath it. Three months earlier I had
watched—not really watched but rather peeked at through my
fingers as a child might at a horror movie—Texas lose the Series
in the most horrific manner. This must be a response to that, I
thought. Like mourning. Like processing with the image of the
dead. Or maybe not exactly that but obligated in that way, to

carry out into the street, into the ordinary life with which it merges very tenderly, I noticed, as he reached to take the baby, long-sleeved undershirt in baseball style extending. Look at that, I thought. How all that baseball stuff extends to all that precious, ordinary other. Look how baseball seems to gather all our hopes unto itself without self-consciousness, apology or error on a beautiful Sunday morning in the garden of the Dream Cafe. "So what is 'OBP'?" I wanted to know. I leaned across to ask—to go right at the heart of things, I figured, since the big home-plate-shaped shield on SaberBoy's hypertrophic chest bore these initials in a fat and friendly calligraphic font that made me guess some sort of dietary supplement. But no. "On-base percentage," I was informed. Ah, yes. Of course. Of course. The wind that lifted SaberBoy's cape behind him so dramatically did not affect his hair. He gazed straight out through black-framed spectacles exactly like the ones Dave England wore. "So"—I leaned over again; I think the baby had, by then, been handed back—"So, tell me . . ." And right here I can't remember how I phrased it, how I formed the question, even what the question was exactly. Something to do with loss, the way the Rangers lost it, twice a single pitch away from winning it all—in case you missed it, *twice.* Just how to carry that along, I guess. What happens to devotion. Everything that it attaches to. And here again I can't recall his answer, only the manner of it—unembarrassed, straight out. How the sun emerged behind him from behind the hazy, scudding morning clouds and how he actually wept a bit and wiped his eyes behind his spectacles, confused perhaps. But altogether unembarrassed. As if it were an allergy or something he was used to. Something chronic, unavoidable.

Today, another Sunday, I'm to meet with Dave again. We live on opposite sides of the city so he picked a public ballpark pretty close to the halfway point. Last week I drove out there to have a look. They're nice fields—four fields actually, numbered one and two and five and six. I didn't see the others. But those four are well maintained. The rust-red baseball dirt is clean and cleanly chalked. Signs stress the need for reservations. There are bleachers. That was Friday and I had it to myself. A couple of cyclists. Someone working on his car. Nobody playing, though, so I just walked around.

———

I SUPPOSE IT MIGHT BE SAD because there's so much standing around and waiting. Guys positioned out there, waiting pretty much like people everywhere. You're standing out there wait-ing, so your thoughts—I'm guessing, surely, at some level—naturally tend to spread back out into the ordinary world. At least a bit. There's some uncertainty on the field. The catcher wants to have a private conversation with the pitcher. Batter's stepping out of the box. But that's okay. We've nothing else to do. These specialized conditions start to seem a little hazy in the hazy afternoon. It is a semipermeable membrane. Thoughts leak out and leak back in. It's like you're standing out in the middle of the whole wide world and waiting for the worst to happen. Here's the world, here's you, and what's about to hap-pen is to happen, start to happen, at the smallest and most con-centrated point of least control. Right off the bat.

———

SO NOW IT'S SUNDAY and I'm here a little early; there he is, though, by the backstop in his Texas Rangers cap. He's got a ball and glove. I should have brought my glove. It's just a softball glove, but still. And, once again, nobody else around. I should have brought a bat. We could have got some serious sadness going

here, at least on my part. "Hey," we say. Shake hands. It's perfect. Everything. The empty fields, the day, the breeze at body
temperature. A center fielder, say, could wait around out there
forever in a kind of equilibrium. I guess everyone's at church.
Memorial Day tomorrow, Dave suggests. They're probably getting ready for Memorial Day. He tosses the ball and catches it in
his glove. Then takes the ball and holds it, turns it in his hand.
Again and again the toss and catch and contemplation. A line
of trees and scattered shrubs contain the outfield imprecisely.
You can see the tops of houses just beyond. It must get touchy
making plays out there where the boundary seems so fuzzy.

So, where's SaberBoy? He'd told me he'd be wearing that
again but instead it's the face of hope, Yu Darvish, our new
pitcher, whose Iranian-Japanese good looks are clearly made
for T-shirt iconography. They've got him down already. Schematized in white on blue above the declaration "Yu is my
homeboy." Yet another variant of the Jesus one. But here it
goes straight Buddhist. Naked-shouldered, arms extended open-
palmed. Khmer bodhisattva just awakened from serenity to
smile at us. It's perfect. All is perfect. All is suffering. I must say
that's just about the rattiest glove I've ever seen. He holds it up.
His dad's, he says. I take some pictures. It's a Franklin Sling-
back, model number 4083. He says his father, Bobby England,
second baseman, won the Dallas City Championship in eighth
grade, back in 1958 or '59. The glove is probably from the seventies. Needs to be restrung, he says. I'd say so. That's about as
broken in as a glove can get, I'd say. Well past that oil-stained
point of confident utility, extending toward the purely philosophical.

So. Here we are on the tiny-wildflowered grass between
fields five and six. We're standing out in the sun, it's getting
warm, but there's a breeze and you can see pretty well from

here the way the fields are all laid out. So where are three and four, I wonder. Huh. He looks around and shrugs. He's just turned forty but seems younger. Fortieth season for the Rangers too. He smiles. He's been to seventeen straight opening days. Sometimes he sleeps with baseball stuff—a glove or a ball or something—under his pillow for good luck. To bring the Texas Rangers luck. He's kept a photograph, he says, of Nelson Cruz not making that catch. Oh yeah, that catch. Game six. I'd put that out of my mind. Boy, when it's time to lose—you know? He does. He knows. I keep expecting Sunday backyard barbecue smells to drift across. But that's tomorrow. They're all waiting, holding off until tomorrow—all those people in those houses you can see beyond the trees, beyond the outfield. Rules get hazy. Thoughts drift in and out. He seems to be okay with this. Just standing out here. All my generalities, not knowing what to ask. He'd probably be okay with hanging around out here all afternoon. His wife, Joanna, will be fine at home with Cooper. That's the baby. Cooper. Cooperstown, you know. The toss, the catch, the contemplation. I can ask whatever I want.

SANTA IN ANATOLIA

———

TWO YEARS AGO, ON A TOUR DESCRIBED BY THE SPONSORING (and financing) Gülen Movement as an encouragement to intercultural dialogue, as well as a way to save a lot of money, Nancy and I found ourselves traveling with a group of friends in Turkey. I had thought to finish a novel there. The novel, titled *Santa Claus*, concerned a failed cartoonist who, in middle age, begins to suffer nightmares of the sort he'd always had as a child at Christmas. But the story had curled in upon itself, self-meditated as it were, to the point where it needed to expand, to get this poor cartoonist out of the house, into the wide historical world—to Turkey, say, where the legends of Saint Nicholas originate. Let him seek the mystery there, I thought, right out in the open, out there by the Aegean in the glare of one of those Pasolini long shots, I imagined, like the ones in his *Medea,* where the narrative might withdraw in a way to leave him stricken, blinded by some awful realization I felt certain we'd discover on our tour.

But it would not work out that way. I'd get back home and write it up and it would hang there like some Lowell Thomas travelogue appended to the feature presentation. I would find

I'd written past the proper claustrophobic ending, and I'd have this little journal full of wonders that no longer spoke to anyone but me. That left me out there in pursuit of an idea I'd sought to delegate. How strange to find yourself—to turn around in a way and find yourself in retrospect—exposed. It makes a difference taking all that in directly. Standing out there in the ruins getting sunburned on your own. No hat, no shades, no cover story. Noon at Ephesus is blinding, for example. All that marble like a mirror. Bleached-white history like a mirror to the blazing here and now. So here's your long shot. There's no Santa, you suspect. Yet here's your notebook and you know where this is leading. You're just not sure what it means.

———

TWO YEARS AGO—TO THE DAY almost; ten days from now it makes two years—we all checked in to a small hotel in Istanbul. Or maybe not so small; I've got a card here, pasted in: Grand Anka Hotel, it says. It didn't seem so grand. A tiny lobby, shadowy hallways, rudimentary rooms. Compressed but nice enough. You felt inserted. And the windows opened. How about that. A sense, at last, of actual air, of openness of place after a fourteen-hour flight into the big end of the funnel of the ancient world then swirled past all that perfectly established ancient scenery that I remember rendering in black-construction-paper silhouette in third grade, down into the tributary avenues increasingly complex with life specific and approachable until, no room for gawking anymore, no distance from it, there you are, squeezed into the narrow end of things, straight through and up into your quarters with a view onto the alley. This is it, you think. A sigh. A pause. And then the windows open. It's the alley, sure. But still. My journal entry:

ISTANBUL, HOTEL ANKA 7-12-10 7:15PM Room window
opens onto orange wall across the alley. Clear, empty evening sky still bright. Sounds of conversation, sounds of
birds echoing in the narrow two-story gap between the
buildings—then crows or something angry-sounding.
Terrible echoy [sic] racket from nowhere in particular, no
visible source, for a couple of seconds. Then just faint,
ambient sounds of the city. Nancy in the bathroom. It's
the Grand Anka Hotel, actually—Molla Gürani Caddesi No.: 46 Findikzade www.grandankahotel.com I'm
drinking a Fanta orange soda as I write this.

Now, this really does feel odd to quote myself, to [sic] myself, but I think this is how you do it, looking back like this—
two years seems long enough to keep its distance and allow
enough uncertainty to fill the gap, to warrant reexamining the
evidence as if there's something there almost like history, by
itself worth looking into. I have a photograph right here that
Nancy took of me, emerging from the bathroom with her sur-
reptitious camera. I'd not seen it till the other day. But there I
am. Backlit and slightly blurred against the orange light through
the window. Pen in hand. A can of Fanta on the little plastic
table. You can see one of the blue-framed vertical window pan-
els open just a little on the right. While on the left I block the
view so you can't see if that one's open, but the gauzy drapes
behind me seem to move. Look how I'm hunched above the
table. Such a strange, sweet Fanta soda–colored light. Am I
aware of that? I wonder. What a strange, sweet light that is? I
probably need to go to bed. But there I am. Ten minutes more
to jot this down, we'll go to bed, awake refreshed more or less,
and set out on this madly overscheduled tour our hosts with

the mysterious Gülen Movement have arranged. Everything will open up again. We'll all be out in the glare and squinting around at everything. But look how things have narrowed to this point—and what a strange, false light to sit and listen into. Sounds in alleys probably always tend to sound, in a way, historical, residual like the ocean in a shell. But here, my goodness, in this light like cartoon sunset, orange-construction-paper sunset to be placed behind the black-construction-paper silhouette of domes and minarets and all that blinded history going back as far as you like. Right back to the origins of windows onto alleys, I imagine. Clatter of dishes. Angry crows.

———

I STILL DON'T QUITE KNOW what the Gülen Movement is. It's either a broad and loosely structured organization that encourages education and intercultural understanding or a subtle plan to Islamize the world. And if the latter, all the more sinister as it looks just like the former. But if the former, how to explain the apparent fervor and devotion of its estimated millions of supporters—all these restaurateurs, hoteliers, private families, news and cultural organizations who'll receive us, charge us nothing, give us fancy Turkish tea sets, Iznik plates in velvet boxes, paper-marbling demonstrations (three or four of these at least)? You'd think a program founded on goals so clearly laudable they might readily find expression in a Miss America pageant wouldn't excite much more than general approbation. Much less fervor. Much less all expenses paid and all this loot. And, to be sure, there will be those among us not so easily charmed, who will regard their fancy tea sets with suspicion. But I'm easy. Easily charmed and lured from caution with a handshake and a box of Turkish delights. The rose-flavored kind. Besides, I like these guys. Our two main guys. Our guides.

Our fervent guides with unpronounceable names, advanced degrees in science—yeah, there's something going on here—and their steady, slightly frantic sense of humor.

I don't even mind the forced march; we were warned about the schedule. It's an inculcating schedule. Inculcation is the order of the day. And every day. For good or evil we're to see the sights, by God, and meet the people. All the sights and very nearly all the people, it would seem. And every bit of it requires complete attention. Looking back to check the record, all the stuff I filtered out because it didn't fit the story, I don't want to miss a thing. There is no story. I will just shut up and read my notes and take my inculcation like a man. Just be a tourist. Just say thank you, do that little hand-to-the-heart thing and be grateful for the marbled-paper samples and the candy and the tea sets. So much kinder, after all, than the alternatives—the fearful things and hateful things like whipping sticks or underwear or coal.

————

RIGHT OFF THE BAT I think I spot a trace, a ghost, an afterimage almost. This is both too easy and too strange. It's our first day. Our first full day and we've already been to breakfast at a famous old café above the Golden Horn. (Though not before a couple of us get lost in a nearby cemetery, wonderfully overgrown, haphazardly terraced into the cliff with leaning monuments of stone or cast concrete atop which turbans or other status-bearing headgear of various types are represented and that look like tailors' forms to hang a coat or a cloak upon. Other vertical slabs of gentler and more undulating style, perhaps once floral in design, have worn away until they look like Halloween children wearing sheets—a pair of sad-eyed fenestrations at the top through which, it occurs to me now, I should have thought to

look, like one of those children, like an imitation spirit. Bend and
lean with the stone to gaze out over the Golden Horn through
the eyes of the Ottoman dead.) Then after breakfast off to the
gaudily modern offices of the daily, Gülen-sympathetic newspaper, *Zaman,* for a tour and a panel discussion of matters cultural
and political and, to me at least, opaque. All this and before the
day is over we shall have penetrated ancient Ottoman tunnels,
paid a visit to the Jewish Museum, a former synagogue . . .

    . . . whose entrance is achieved down such a narrow
    passage past such a clutter of shops and small concerns
    and up such an odd little twisting stair at the end, you
    wonder if it tells, still, of a protective obscurity.

And whose contents—photos, clothing, old religious items
mostly—seem to preserve that small and precious vulnerability
of objects just unwrapped, removed from a family trunk, and
all beneath a pale blue ceiling painted, as if by a careful child,
with uncertain ranks of gold stars. We shall have plied the Bosporus up and down in a passenger ferry and, finally, toured an
art school in a gutted, hastily modernized former palace by the
water where we all sit outside for a while and watch the shadows spread and find ourselves amused and maybe comforted a
little by the attentions of a small orange cat. But right in the
middle of this, our first full day, and right at noon and right in
the center of the city as we're all processing—more like being
herded; we are thirteen—down the Istiklal Caddesi, Istanbul's
great central avenue, I stop to look where Nancy's pointing, up
at a clear blue sky, to see a trace of Santa there, a cartoon scribble made of wire and neon tubing dangling way up there from
a cable or a power line we see is part of an elevated grid of
lines and cables running the whole length of the Istiklal Cad-

desi to provide, I guess, support for needs both practical and ritual. A dormant neon snowflake farther on, another Santa or a snowman—hard to tell. They are so faint here in the middle of July, these wintry images like dreams, like racial memory drifting down from who knows where into this vast protective net above the back-and-forth of ordinary life.

———

SO, HOW WOULD LOWELL THOMAS navigate all this? In an easy, jovial way, I'm sure. Don't get too serious or you're bound to run 'em off. But not so differently, I think, from Pasolini. Under all that joviality Thomas's camera tends to start and gape as we would; in the early documentaries especially, they've not learned quite yet to separate the camera's gaze from ours. It's still a little like home movies. Mostly long shots. Our attention tends to wander from the narrative just as Pasolini seems to want it to—to sense the place where the story hovers like a mist or a cloud of dust kicked up, an accident, just barely there for a while, just sort of hanging in the ordinary air, odd bits detaching, drifting off.

———

THE POINT IS, FINALLY, to reach Demre, ancient Myra, on the southern coast of Turkey, where Saint Nicholas, to whatever extent, existed. Where his legends concentrate and his church still stands. But that's a week or so away and there's a lot of ground to cover, all these other points to touch upon. To try to keep in mind. I can remember having those terrible dreams myself on Christmas Eve when I was a kid. I think I probably always had them. It was part of the deal—you had to make it through. All night to wake again and again convinced that you'd misunderstood somehow. That you had got it wrong, completely wrong and in the morning you would find yourself unwrapping—such a precious, vulnerable thing to have to do in any case, to have to kneel beneath the tree, remove the ribbon and the paper— but you'd find yourself unwrapping nothing much. You'd find that there was really nothing much at all. How worse than nothing that can be. You can't imagine. So, you'd shake it off and try to go back to sleep but it would be like that till morning. Nancy says she and her brothers never quite got what they wanted. Which is not the same at all. To be expecting the Lone Ranger and get Tonto, long for Barbie and get Midge (I never even heard of "Midge." Who gives their daughter "Midge" for Christmas?), but that's still okay. Midge represents, at least, the higher order. The transcendent possibility inheres. I had to wonder, though, if she had ever thought to be perverse and ask for Midge to see if, maybe, she'd get Barbie. No, she said. We never did. We didn't want to *not* believe. Which is exactly what she said. She didn't want to not believe.

———

THE FOUR GREAT HIGHER-ORDER ANGELS gazing down from under the dome of Hagia Sophia are of that complicated many-winged variety that has always seemed so strange to me—so tangled yet compelling, as the record of some garbled close encounter and the iconographic struggle to make sense of it. Like Antoine Sonrel's amazing scientific illustration of the gazillion-tentacled jellyfish *Cyanea arctica,* less about what's there than what's required to make it graspable at all. These mosaic angels seem as freshly, forcibly drawn into reluctant comprehension as some creature never seen before hauled straight up from the depths, laid on the deck, exploded, wrecked and uninterpretable—each one a somewhat differently contorted blast of feathers as if captured in a net, pulled from the vacuum down, in this case, into regions so compressed and dense with

longing there is little left to deal with but distortion, this im-
plosion of desire to be addressed as best we can, with no less
care than if it were a scientific illustration. Nancy thinks at first
they're "thrones," among the most exalted angels. Later on deciding "seraphim," the highest of them all. The ranks of angels
seem as grand, obscure, and powerful as those of champagne
bottle sizes. Potent with a certain risk, you sense from restora-
tions under way on one of the angels, who's been opened, as it
were—his gold Islamic cover taken off to show the fourteenth-
century Christian face, which looks not altogether pleased to
be let out into the thin ambivalent air.

Then on to the Blue Mosque. No ambivalence here. Maintained in its original serenity. One's presence does not echo.
There is carpet and a single hushed uncomplicated thought to
fill the complicated, ornamental space the way time occupies
the clockwork. Curiosity seems, here, beside the point, and so
do we. I don't even think to look, as earlier, for ancient names
in Greek or runes carved into the marble. Here we simply take
our shoes off, stand around, and get absorbed. A little later,
at Topkapi, I'm still wearing the little gold-embroidered Turkish cap I had bought from one of the vendors outside Hagia
Sophia. I refuse to remove it though I know it's silly. At some
point, at a famous photographic prospect with the Bosporus
far below, I strike a pose and announce that I am David Pasha
and that everyone's to call me David Pasha, and they do and
I am gratified and inexplicably happy to be wearing my silly
cap of orange-red velvet embroidered with gold and set with
pearls and bits of mirror. I sense I've got myself caught up in
something. In this silly tourist business—in the seriousness of
it, thinking after all this is quite serious, this is how one goes
about becoming Chatwin, Burton, Thesiger, whoever I imagine
in exotic circumstances. This is what a silly hat is all about: you

must give in to it, cast your dignity aside, allow yourself to be ridiculous and take your pose at the wall above the Bosporus, but a pose—one must be careful here—constrained to a degree of self-awareness, to so subtle an adjustment of the gesture, of the foolishness, the obviousness of posing in a fancy hat above the sweep of history, so receptive to the simple invitation of the moment that the faintest sense of truth, dare I suggest, creeps in, to everyone's amusement and surprise. Which I receive as confirmation (as a child puts on his costume to become whatever he wants, become the pretense which at that age he can sense is only slightly less believable than being here at all) that I am truly David Pasha, have become him in some barely meaningful way; that one can do this, find one's place, as it were, in history, all this ornamental history, through such ornament and foolishness— just step right into what, in fact, seems hardly less believable than being here at all. As we are gathering to leave, a young, attractive Turkish couple I'd not noticed on our tour but who, I have to think, had been observing us, nod, smile, and call me David Pasha as they pass and I am overcome with joy.

———

THE FOLLOWING DAY WE take a high-speed ferry across the Sea of Marmara to Bursa. I love that. It seems a marvelous thing to say. The Sea of Marmara. This gives me an hour or so to catch up on my journal. Nancy moves to the windows. Then outside to the rail, where she remains for the rest of our passage.

Three days later in the little Cappadocian town of Göreme, as I find myself surrendered (as I'd promised not to do) to childhood-Christmas-style intensity of longing toward the gorgeous village weavings you see hanging everywhere, I allow myself (like some poor old conventioneer alone at night on Bourbon Street) to pass beyond the threshold into regions of

desire, into the ancient Silk Road carpet shop of the world presided over by a figure straight from Bourbon Street, to start the
ancient, wary conversation:

> Any old ones? Sure. And quickly I can see that there are
> old ones, room after room. And this? This dandy little
> piece . . . draped over a chair? Nomadic. Gorgeous color.
> Bright surprizing [sic] pattern. . . . 300 dollars. Really?
> Okay, you have good eye—nice old piece 250. Shit. 250.
> Now I'm really lost and taken into back rooms. Holy
> moly. Some of these I've seen in books. This looks like
> Ghiordes. "Good"—he shakes my hand—"almost; it's
> from that area." Then a brilliant one way back there in
> the corner hanging up. A prayer rug . . . Beautiful red
> mihrab, green field, the borders clear, unfussy. "Good
> condition. From a mosque." I catch his eye and smile;
> at this point I am reckless—"I suppose that's what
> you say." He lifts his head, goes stern—"I bought the
> mosque. Ten thousand for the mosque. This rug has
> never been on floor."

So, as all this transpires, and I emerge with my purchase,
Nancy sees and understands, from her watchful distance, how
I do, how I can lose peripheral vision, eyes locked into goofy
spirals. And that night presents an antidote, a vision like a Pasolini long shot. (How did she know to wait to save it?) She tells
how, as we were coming across on the ferry, as she stood there
at the rail gazing over the gentle azure surface, she observed,
some distance away, a little carpet all spread out, just floating
along on the Sea of Marmara. Inexplicable, beautiful, vanishing thing out there all by itself. A little dream of a little Oriental
carpet.

We go shopping. We have lunch. We visit a mosque. Shoes off, shoes on. I get silly again at an ancient kebab house—the Bursakebapcisi—folding an airplane from a beautifully imprinted vellum place mat and releasing it from a second-story window into the courtyard among the diners. A satisfactory, slightly stalling, circling flight to the waiters' great, and no doubt feigned, appreciation. There's no story. There's no novel. I can do whatever I want. I think the condition of the tourist must be pretty close to that of the hysteric. It's the open-ended wideness of the world sensed as a fact unto itself that makes us crazy. Then more shopping. Then a rush of conversation between our guides, a couple of phone calls. We're about to go off-schedule, slip beneath the subtle membrane that protects our presence here. Tonight, not far away although we'll have to hurry, an unadvertised, unglamorized performance of the whirling Sufic ecstasies.

. . . at the tiny "House of Saint Karabash"—Dervishes. It would put us very late on our long bus ride to Izmir, but a rare opportunity to see a simple unspectacularized performance at an ordinary place enjoyed by ordinary people. So, after supper, after dark, we make our way up narrow rough-stone streets to the mosque-like House of Karabash and outside under little lights [strung] here and there in the trees were families, children, neighborhood people probably, settled gently into the evening at picnic tables, children running around and everything quite easy as we file into the house, remove our shoes and take our places—women upstairs with the better view I think . . . [men] on the carpeted floor behind a balustrade. And after fifteen minutes or so, the Sufis— maybe a dozen—[appear] in their black robes and their

tall felt caps (and two of them, the leaders, wearing caps
with rolls of green cloth at the bottom . . .) and after
the placing of a red-stained sheepskin to one side of the
performance space, the chanters along the wall begin to
chant, the drummers drum their tambourines, the flut-
ers flute and the whirlers (five, I think) take off their
black to reveal their pure white whirling gowns and so,
at the sad descending groan of the older of the leaders,
start to turn, to the flute and the chant, like an orrery
out on the floor—a young one, maybe 10 or 12 I'd guess,
with the face of an Italian Renaissance angel, among the
five, a minor planet but in perfect, measured orbit circulating at a steady but, one senses, potent rate as if, *Boléro*-
like, it had the capability of frenzy. At some point it all
jacks up, but just a bit, speeds up a third, and they're all
circulating out there, eyes closed, each rotating on his
axis as all circle about the center into which the portly,
bearded older leader has now placed himself, his eyes
closed too and turning but in black still, an invisible at-
tractor (you remember how, at the start, each whirler
came to sort of lean into him gently for a moment as if
taking on his gravity), now he's there as if to hold them
in as things speed up and somewhere—I can't find the
source—a punctuating cry, a deep expulsion of breath,
to each phrase of the chant and you think we're in for it
now—we, gathered here so easily to watch, those looking in from the open door, the ones outside in the summer evening hanging out beneath the trees and the little
lights, we're really in for it now. But suddenly they stop.
All five at once. The little one too. Just as we're made to
understand it can, in principle, go on and on and faster
and faster forever, they all stop without a shudder or a

stumble, even the little angel-faced one. They are able to seem to have come to a perfect stop because, in principle, they haven't stopped at all. Then back in the bus and on to Izmir through the night. I think about something Nancy said regarding that gasping Sufic cry and how she thought such cries were the name of Allah reduced to the act of breathing, to the sound of breath released and that she'd read somewhere that Yahweh (Jaweh?) as the name of God had come from breath, from such a gasping cry. We get into Izmir and check into the Marlight Hotel at 4am. I think of poor Professor Miller on Mt. Wilson back in the 20s with his giant interferometer hoping to catch the breath of the luminiferous ether on his perfectly polished mirrors like the breath of God—if not the word then maybe just the breath.

Until the famous Michelson-Morley experiment in 1887, it was generally thought that the "vacuum" of space was filled with an unimaginably subtle fluid called the luminiferous ether, which provided both a means for the otherwise inexplicable propagation of light across the void and for a certain level of comfort with the emptiness. So deeply, amniotically sustaining was this notion, some refused to let it go, to accept the negative results from the beams of light bounced back and forth within an arrangement of little mirrors in a basement room in Cleveland.

Dayton Miller believed the experiment too earthbound. How could ether—were it present and of course it must be present—so imponderable, almost spiritual a substance, manage to penetrate that mundane situation, drift through dirt and brick to breathe upon the massive and, in any case, inconclusive apparatus? And though special relativity, in a few years, would reveal the ether itself to have been a mundane and unnecessary mechanism, Miller would pursue it into the twenties, finally assembling what was believed to be the most sensitive interferometer in the world atop Mount Wilson and installing it in an airy, tentlike structure way up there as near to heaven as he could get so that the ether might drift right through like a breeze or the Holy Spirit on a summer night at some old tent revival, and contriving, after something like five million separate measurements, to hear, to believe he heard, within the sighings and the creakings of it all, within the "noise" of human, thermal, and mechanical uncertainty, the reassuring whisper of earth's passage through the dark. It was not audible to others, though. Experiments could not confirm his data, which, years later, were submitted to modern analytical methods and found to have been entirely consistent with a negative result—a kind of rigorous wishful thinking. Photographs show a strong, kind face. He was devoted to his family. Played the flute. And I imagine him up there with this great instrument physically, personally having to turn it through its stations all those months, like wetting a finger to find the wind but over and over through the seasons, turning and turning toward the longed-for absolute.

———

WE ARE AT EPHESUS AT NOON. It's like I said. Like a mirror. It's 100 degrees outside, someone will tell me later. Something's happened to my camera; I've reset it accidentally or something, or it's somehow overloaded. All the pictures overexposed, burned out—exactly how I feel. We've advanced beyond the black-construction-paper silhouette, beyond the Fanta-colored sunset into the light of history. Bleached-white, ruined-marble history, which is blinding. Look about you. All is glare. That tired old bleached-out dusty hound over there is fading as we watch. He's part of history. Aren't you, boy. He's found a patch of shade among the scattered stones and fallen columns. He's a sad old ruined marble dog. There's hardly any shade. So history's just a sort of overexposure, isn't it, boy. He knows. He's fine with that.

Then off to a rug shop where they teach young girls to weave and I escape without a purchase. Then, as evening falls, a Gülen-inspired high school, where we get a demonstration of the art of paper marbling. Most impressive are the ink-on-water tulips. Ink on water has a physics that's agreeable to tulips. And to tourists, I surmise. We get more marbled-paper tulips the following day at a Gülen— What to say? Gülen-inspired? Encouraged? It's all good. I am encouraged. I love tulips. Anyway, a somehow Gülen-affiliated hospital, where we all receive, as well, hand-painted porcelain plates in dark blue velvet boxes and our names, if we wish, in calligraphic felt-tip-marker Arabic. My goodness, is that me? My name as beautiful as that? As easy as that? We don't deserve this. We'll only take it home and put it away, years later come across it, take it out again and think, Well, look at that. That's something, isn't it. All that stuff. That's really something, I suppose.

Did you know Gülen himself—Fethullah Gülen, the septuagenarian Muslim scholar and founder of the movement— lives in the Poconos? Pennsylvania. On a private estate in the Poconos. Well, he does. At such a strange remove, it seems, from his effect. Menachem Schneerson—known as the Lubavitcher Rebbe and, by many of his followers, believed to be the Messiah—lived in Brooklyn. Buried in Queens. The Messiah. All right here at home. So here again, you see, it's the clear and empty wideness of the world that lets our longing fill it up, spread out to the edge like ink on water, makes us crazy.

It's an hour's flight to Kayseri, whose exuberantly futuristic City Museum suggests to me some sort of interstellar conveyance and, to Nancy, one of those Transformer toys about to unfold into a giant robot. Or the fanciest imaginable 1980s boom box. Or an attempt to schematize the unearthly erosional shapes of the Cappadocian landscape, toward which we, in fact, depart the following day on a lurching bus ride west to Göreme and the tufa "fairy chimneys" and the ancient human-excavated villages and monasteries. Nearly there we pass a small encampment by the road—a battered car beneath a tree, three improvised tents. I joke that they're Gypsies. But they are. They come through here a lot, we're told. How about that. Gypsies. Periodically, like swallows.

In this region frescoed angels tend to populate the caves instead of bats. There may be bats as well, and pigeons too, but mostly there are angels, saints, and Christs in full array. The whole developed kit of heaven has gone strangely underground. Between the eighth and fourteenth centuries, all that radiant iconography seems to have percolated right back into the rock like geode crystals. Whence it came, I guess, if you go back far enough. The excavations by the British archaeologist James Mellaart in the early sixties at Çatalhöyük, only a hundred miles from here, revealed an urbanizing, Neolithic culture dating back eight thousand years, complete with shrines, including sculptural and painted iconography, within which, here and there, were bits of evidence suggesting even older, deeper gropings toward the sacred in the natural shapes of pebbles and concretions, broken pieces of stalagmite that presented to the clear and credulous mind dark hints of power and fecundity— rude subterranean forms sometimes improved by a quick and, one imagines, trepidatious hand (an especially "fearful"

and perfunctory human head pecked out atop a blackened "knobbly limestone" lump), touched up to keep the terrible potency in focus and, perhaps, in check.

Outside one of the subterranean churches filled with angels, in the lime-white glare of the afternoon, you can barely see, in the rock, outlines of hands. At first just two or three— left hands—scored into the tufa with a knife or a nail like a child might do with a crayon using his own hand, fingers spread into a template. Then you start to see them everywhere—all over the clear pale rock with the sun just bright enough to wash the natural texture out yet show the marks, the fainter and fainter outlines, older and older, even overlapping, merging into one another until the pressure of the hands against the rock becomes the texture and you can't not see them—as if they were wanting to get into the church, wanting something, frantic almost, marking not so much where hands were placed as where they lost their grip and slipped away.

I'm out of Band-Aids, having used them all to mask the inexplicably bright blue light that seems, in every hotel room so far, to call our attention, through closed eyelids all night long, to the fact that the TV is still powered up and waiting to be turned on. Perhaps it's meant to reassure—a sort of penetrating night-light meant to tell us not to worry about bad dreams and let us know that there is always a means at hand to take our minds off things like that. But here at last in our little cave hotel in Göreme—it's okay. The light is red. No need for a Band-Aid. Red is fine here in our humid semisubterranean room carved out of rock. It's like an eye. A tiny, ancient, red interrogating eye. Is Santa here? Nearby somewhere? 'Tis said he knows when we are sleeping or awake. It's back to Istanbul tomorrow, where we'll catch a flight to Antalya, on the Mediterranean coast. At which point Nancy and I part company with the others for the day and take a hired car south along the coast to Demre.

We are told it's best to hire a car. It is a coastal road but the mountains come right down to the ragged edge of the Mediterranean. There are tunnels, lots of turns and switchbacks, places where the eye will leave the road. Where all of a sudden there's the water. There's the blue you get in children's paintings. Blue as that primordial blue you've had in mind since childhood.

You approach the travel office from the sidewalk; there's a little sliding window like a snow-cone stand. We wait as our guide for the day, who neither drives nor speaks much English, seeks to establish our requirements, general worthiness, or something. This takes time. We're finally beckoned to a side door, down some stairs into a semibasement room, and given tea. A heavy man in a crisp white short-sleeved shirt sits at his desk and speaks for a moment with our guide, who also wears a crisp white short-sleeved shirt. He turns to us and tells us it will be three hundred lira. Or about two hundred dollars, which is fine. I place the cash in American dollars on the desk. The heavy man leans back. We're waiting. For our driver, I presume—who must be summoned or retrieved. It takes a while. We have our tea. The oscillating fan across the room lifts Nancy's hair. At last a clatter from the stairwell and a third white short-sleeved figure peeks in, smiles, holds open the door to admit another, smaller, darker, whose white short-sleeved shirt seems placed a little hastily upon him like a coat of fresh white paint to cover up some old graffito that persists in bleeding through. His eyes are bright. His ears are large. His skull is shallow as a begging bowl. Great scrawl of a nose to compensate, to keep him pointed straight into the wind across the steppe, across the ages. Now we're set. The fan whirs back and forth. The heavy man can't seem to find the keys.

On the mountainous road to Demre . . . there are pine trees. "Look," says Nancy, "Christmas trees." The road climbs up and in and out among the rocky Colorado-looking hills. We lose the shore for a while, then gradually after an hour or so dip down and back to find the complex edge of the deep blue Mediterranean, swerving around the inlets, some of which have cliffs and shallow caves and bathers. Here and there are gauzy quonset huts. Then acres of them—thin white fabric greenhouses. We pass by a giant tomato held aloft in a giant hand—a public monument. The quonset huts are empty though. The ground inside is covered in the same white gauzy cloth. "The earth is sleeping," says our guide for the day who most call Sam although his name is Ufuk. "That's poetic," Nancy says. "Did I say wrong?" asks Ufuk. "No," says Nancy. "No. It is poetic."

It's an active blue somehow. It's almost noon, and the light comes straight down into the water so you get the depth of blue against the limestone white of the shore, which you imagine should dissolve like Alka-Seltzer. Fizz away like history. How can it still be blue like that? How can it not have gotten all used up by now—after thousands of years of myth and history, not been neutralized, gone empty bathwater gray like the Gulf of Mexico, say, where myth has long departed and there's nothing left but fishing trawlers, drillers, and sometimes way out there a tanker, simply going about their business on the gray depleted water. How can it stay that way, you wonder. Blue that holds us in suspension. Wine-dark blue that stands for black. Do you suppose there might be different grades of emptiness? As Cantor claimed for infinities? At about the same time Michelson and Morley sought the ether, Cantor showed, in a very precise sort of way, how there could be greater and lesser infinite sets. How the infinite might, depending on what kind of numbers you used to think about it, have higher or lower "cardinality." Might we not, then, point the arrow the other way, turn all this inside out to imagine something similar for emptiness? A scale of potentiality? Of blueness, as it were? The variable likelihood that, out of nothing, myth will simply happen.

A sign by the road we stop to photograph: a Coca-Cola Santa, old style, sad eyes gazing up as saints' will do, and beckoning us to a local restaurant.

It's the fat, red-suited Santa we all love. The Coca-Cola Santa Claus whose mission and refreshment are the world's. And yet how strange his eyes are here. Their heavenward gaze so sad and saintly, a platter of seafood held before him like the emblem of his martyrdom.

In Demre he is everywhere. Cartoony ones on signs. Greek/Russian icons. Keychains. Postcards. [Everywhere you look are] motor scooters. A gaggle of Russian tourists. Little tractors pulling wagonloads of melons—some adorned with carefully handmade canvas covers—tractor cozies—over the engine cowl and headlights. One, of faded blue, has decorative scarlet zig-zag appliqué around the edges. Then the owner, at my interest, comes to stand beside it, lets me take his picture.

Where's the church? Where is the seat of Holy Nicholas? Our driver spots a sign. Just down the street. It's hot. Cicadas

chatter everywhere. Not quite a Texas chatter. Slightly deeper,
lower frequency. Once noticed, it's oppressive. All the motor
scooters too—in such an ancient holy place they seem like temple monkeys. We decide it's lunchtime. Here's the Noel Baba
Restaurant. Seafood platters, if you please. We sit outside. The
garish signage features cartoon Santas. One of whom is listening to something, a wide-eyed Santa with a mitten to his ear. To
what, I wonder, is he listening? To the motor scooters maybe?
The cicadas? I think maybe the cicadas.

There's no church. I see no church. Its iterations—sixth to
eighth to eleventh to nineteenth centuries—ought to be piled
up right here one on top of another. A great conspicuous,
reverential heap. The hopes and fears of all the years. The alter-
nating levels. Midge and Barbie. Love. Despair. The Russian
tourists seem to know where they are going. Sure enough,
there is an entrance to the grounds. And here's a company of
stray dogs to admit us. All these holy sites have complements
of animals, it seems. I love the wonderfully important-looking
tickets you're issued at these places by the Ministry of Culture.
I collect them for my journal. I imagine they're expensive to
produce, each with its site-specific photograph and shimmery
silver seal and whatever that is—that black magnetic strip, I
guess—there at the bottom. Every photograph of every site—
full color, at the left below the ministry name and logo—has
been taken in the clear, bright afternoon. Blue sky, a wisp of
cloud. The past, once clearly identified in ordinary light, seems
easy as anyplace to get to. Here we are, then. There's a gift
shop. Benches set about. A great bronze statue of a European
"Father Christmas" Santa with the children of the world around
his feet. I've got a picture of our driver on a bench—he and
our guide prefer to wait outside the church, which by the
way seems more like a working excavation, down a ramp and

partially covered by a huge protective awning; I am told the sea was nearer then, the land much lower; now it looks subsided, unprepared for this attention, just dug up; who would have thought, look what we've found—but anyway, I've got this photograph of Dogan (from his name tag, I'm not sure how it's pronounced) in his crisp white shirt, his loosened tie, black trousers, water bottle dangling from his hands between his knees. (I ought to tell you, very quickly, about the bottled water here. I've saved a label Nancy peeled; the brand is "Sandras." Sandras water. Did you know as late as Hellenistic times they minted silver coins with the image of an ancient deity worshipped here and hereabouts called Santa, Sandan, or Sandas? And that on these coins he's shown atop a pyre where he was burned at annual festivals. And afterward his resurrection and ascension celebrated. How about that. Right up the chimney as it were. You see how complicated all this starts to be.) So anyway, as I keep saying— anyway, I've got this photograph of Dogan, our driver, sitting on a bench outside the church near the top of the ramp. He smiles straight back into the camera. We're about to go inside, walk down the ramp at last—I wish the church were more; it looks much nicer in the photo on our tickets, with grass and flowers, clear of scaffolding and awnings—and I turn to take his picture. He can't help but look eternal—ears of Buddha, face of Pan. A reassuring smile, I think, is what's intended. He'll be here when we come out. But it's the smile of the guy who runs the scary carnival ride. As complex and ambivalent as that.

Inside, the church is clear of all except the deepest ambiguities—going to rubble at the edges but within all dark and open with the fading light of frescoes Nancy says are by a provincial hand (11th century mostly, I think—my little guide book's with my baggage) . . . but a much less polished hand in any case, observant of the protocols, the chant of it all I guess—it feels like that. The matter-of-factness of the miracle. And St. Nicholas matter-of-factly here as well, at least in principle—his marble tomb apparently borrowed from another [worthy somewhere]. He is everywhere—we know that. The cicadas sound like sleighbells.

There are dogs here, too. Two dogs asleep right here in the very center of the nave. Is this the nave? Of course it is. There's someone kneeling at the altar at the far end where the afternoon glares in through arched stone windows. And these dogs, big dogs, a red one and a white one, simply laid out on the cool stone floor. Right out there in the middle. In the novel *Santa Claus,* the one all this does not belong to, wherefrom I have been released to seek the truth on my own account, there is a kid based on a kid I actually knew when I was one. An easily frightened little chubby kid who lived just down the street and whom we'd torment by pretending we could hear, somewhere in the distance, monstrous noises, sounds of Giant Killer Shrews (a recent locally filmed production featuring dogs made up like monsters who produced a terrible, cicada-like chittery cry). And when we did this, he'd run home. He'd drop whatever he was doing and just bolt. I think sometimes he was thrilled. Exhilarated. At those moments when the always-fearful world revealed itself to him so clearly and he knew exactly what was what and what he had to do. One of the dogs is up. The white one. Trotting over now to Nancy. We were told we shouldn't pet them. There's a danger of disease. But she extends her hand. It sniffs and wags and seems to want a pat. Here comes the other one. My goodness, they like Nancy.

They're like beggars importuning. Jumping up and interfering with each other. Now there's trouble. Now we're in for it. Now the Russians turn to look. The red and white are going at it. Just like that. They're at that frenzy, at that sudden full ferocity that takes your breath away. Where's Nancy? Over against the wall. It sucks the air right out. The kneeling lady stands and turns with both hands to her mouth. How cool and dark and clear it is, right here at the heart of things. How clearly things reveal themselves. Who knew? The shady afternoon. The fragmentary frescoes like lace curtains. Everything reducing here into this blur, this swirl, the awful, almost vocalizing roar of it replacing, for a moment, all the space. Replacing everything—the miracle, the saints and the apostles and the angels with their sharp red wings. So terrible, the way it happens just like that, so naturally and easily. And just like that it's over. Dogs withdraw, resume their former life. The light comes in. Cicada sounds. The Russians drift away into their chatter.

At the gift shop I decide to buy a T-shirt—simple dark blue, almost black, with an image of Nicholas's hand in blessing. What comes next sort of fades on out. Three miles away are the ruins of Myra—not the town itself exactly, where Saint Nicholas was bishop, but the older parts, the Roman-era theater and the ancient Lycian necropolis. And the residue, more residue than anything else, I think—assorted capitals and column sections, blocks of stone with carvings and inscriptions—like the items in a junkyard stacked and waiting for a better day. And everywhere on every other stone it seems are carved these gaping archaistic masks. Theatrical masks, their empty eyes and mouths wide open—comic, tragic, worn away to something like astonished. Like bewildered. I suppose they once belonged to a great theatrical facade. But now—as it seems to me, and as I say it seems to fade away—so close beneath the rock-cut tombs on the cliff above they seem like faces of the dead. A few have pebbles in their mouths. I'll ask a member of our company, John Lunsford—my old teacher, former director of the Meadows Museum in Dallas, famous polymath and specialist in everything—about that. If he knows of some tradition that involves the placing of pebbles in the ancient open mouths like that. You think of pebbles left on Jewish graves of course. But he does not. I'll bet it's children. That's exactly what a kid would do. The obvious thing to do. You place a pebble in its mouth. And then what, I would ask the child. Do you stick around? Do you want to hear what he has to say, I'd ask the child who placed the smooth, flat, tongue-shaped pebble there. Would you care to put your ear up close and listen? I'll bet not. You placed the pebble there and ran. A thousand years ago I'll bet that's what you did. I know I would. I'd run straight home. It's getting late. We need to head back pretty soon and Nancy wants to see the beach. We pass a number of the empty, gauzy Quonset huts on the road back into town, but now they're brilliant, incandescent in the angling-reddening sunlight. They all glow. Yes, we have nothing. No tomatoes. No bananas. Yet how radiantly, warmly empty. Back through Demre, past another of those signs with the saintly seafood-laden Santa. The shore arcs way around to the east and out to a postcard point of land. There are no cicadas here, just surf. Ufuk and Dogan stand by the car and have a smoke. Did Lowell Thomas ever just shut up, do you think? Just sort of let the camera run? Nancy has kicked her sandals off. She's wading. We can't stay here long. We've got a schedule for the evening. Now she's standing in the surf and bent a little with her head turned. Beckoning. "Listen." There's the sound of surf but, underneath, something else—a different, deeper, dragging and abrasive sound. The rocks. The pebbles. Here's where all the pebbles come from.

The shore is made of differently colored pebbles and the surf is doing its work. Well, here you go. Here are the voices of the dead. Here's what the cartoon Santa listens for. Of course. So, what do they want? I can't imagine. Nothing much. "Look." Nancy holds some up. They're processed, sorted—all are smooth and flat but with the larger ones on top and smaller and smaller underneath. There is a system here. She scoops a little deeper, brings up smaller ones—all shades of white and gray and brown and black and even red, with different geological histories, I suppose, but processed here into these simple, pretty things that come so easily into the hand. She chooses a few to keep. To take home as mementos. Just to have. Right at the edge of dissolution, beauty comes into the hand. We can't let go.

HOW TO COLOR
THE GRASS

———

I CAN REMEMBER BEING A CHILD AND BEING BLANK. WITHOUT opinion. Walking around like that. Complete like that. All fear and desire with not much in between. I think of it now as an experimental setup. Like a cloud chamber—where you've got this otherwise empty vessel filled with a sort of mist through which events, the passage of subatomic particles, leave evanescent trails. And it kind of felt like a mist, I think. Experience loomed. You tended not to see it coming. All of a sudden there it was. Surprise attached to things quite naturally—a property. "Remarkable," as the only response that toddler in the early "Our Gang" comedies had to anything, made sense. Made people laugh to sense the truth of it. To see it as this monocled astonishment. And all in the course of a day. Here, for example, is a little tabby kitten I remember by the fence. My God. There's never been a thing like this before, I don't believe. A tabby kitten by the fence. And here is Donald—I remember how my mother said it, carefully: *Here's Donald*—not quite potty-trained yet diaperless, from across the street to play in 1950 in the flat and treeless postwar neighborhood where everybody lived. Where is his mother? It's remarkable. A fundamental wonder.

Irreducible and perfect in his saggy shorts against the great simplicity of things.

I'm pretty sure I can remember being able—standing out there in the yard one day and coming to realize that I was able— to count to twenty-four. That's crazy, isn't it. Not your Helen Keller sort of moment. Twenty-four—enough for now. A point of pride. Each number, after all, a world unto itself. There is no structure, no procedure. There are objects in the mist that leave these brief and sometimes pungent little trails.

The fear and desire, of course, are initial conditions, part of the basic setup. Something like the electromagnets that I understand were sometimes used to influence the behavior of those subatomic particles leaving traces in the "cloud." To spin them this way or that depending on their charge. You've got your negative and positive. Your fear and desire. And, certainly, events did seem to deflect one way or the other according to something like a charge. Another property—we're on our way to a unifying theory. So, why muck it up with complicating notions such as long division, grammar, and artistic verisimilitude?

In third grade, Art became a separate class in a separate classroom in the second-oldest and second-dankest wing of our school. Our school preserved these sort of Dantean divisions. Oldest and dankest, from which hope had long departed and where knowledge, like the smell of disinfectant, seemed residual and corrective, was the grim, three-story nineteenth-century section like an orphanage where old, dank Mrs. Gilbert taught arithmetic. At the other end was the new part with the bright, expansive, modernistic promise of improvement and eventual release. But in between, this purgatorial stage. Uncomfortable. Uncertain. Built in the thirties, merely bleak, through which you had to pass to get to either end, and where we found ourselves presented, in the middle of the third grade, with a novel and uncomfortable understanding of the nature of depiction and I guess, therefore, of the world. And which seemed all the more uncomfortable as introduced so patiently and sweetly by so luminous an advocate, so unaccountably kind and clear and young and blond and beautiful a presence as appeared before us there in those bleak circumstances. Let's go out and draw the playground, shall we? If you say so, absolutely. Though it seems a bit direct. So out we march into the sunlight with our crayons, little knowing what's in store, to draw as kids draw, to record the simple axiomatic facts, the green of grass and blue of sky. We had it down. We knew our job. It was an inventory. Knowing what was there. Of course, the knowing was the point. We knew what the playground was. We didn't need to go out there to see. But she was new— had no idea that we could bring it forth out of our understanding in complete, schematic, universal clarity, on request. Whatever she'd like—the moon and stars, our homes and moms and dads and pets. Why should we need to summon Bozo in his doggy specificity? He's established: snout and ears, cigar-shaped body, four straight legs and, if you're John Hernandez, pooping. All John's animals were rendered in the defecatory style. Their pungent trails identified them—since first grade, in fact. By now, no longer funny, it was simple iconography. These qualities emerged and that was that. We understood. Though not advanced, we were internally consistent.

Is there still Manila paper? In those huge impermanent, friable, yellow sheets kept in a stack, to be retrieved upon command. And always called Manila paper? Never just "paper," though there was no other kind for us to use. "Manila" seemed a special qualifier. Spoken to remind us of the deep discardability of all this. We might find ourselves absorbed, get really into it, wind up actually kind of liking what we'd done, but at the end—and even pinned up on display it seemed a little sad, especially in this sad, uncertain region—it was on Manila paper. All the otherwise so clear and convincing qualities of things. We must have sensed it couldn't last.

It was the kindness of it, though, I found most troubling. Oh my, this is very good. Yes, this is lovely. Oh, but look . . . (Old Mrs. Gilbert, drawn to error as a vulture to corruption, would have made it easier, hardened my response to mere obedience.) Oh, but see if you look at the grass, it isn't really solid green like that. You know? (Perhaps I knew. Perhaps in a background sort of way, as one knows there is death and history and other imponderables. But of course it's green. We all know grass is green.) But look. You see? (I didn't really need to look. But here's this angel gently guiding me to look back over ground I thought I'd crossed, transcended, managed to express within a workable idea—am I to toss all that away, go mulch it up, return to unresolved constituents?) See, look. Look at the colors. Look at all the browns and yellows. See if you can draw that, won't you? See if you can try to draw it as it is. (Why should I draw it as it is? We already have it as it is. Why have it twice? And what will John Hernandez do—reduced to realism? All that he's invested. I suspect it will not translate very well.)

One Sunday morning, late in January, I stopped by my old school, parked, and walked across the mostly brown and yellow grass to the rear of the purgatorial section—now the oldest part since, years ago, the orphanage was torn down and replaced by a clean, low, practical structure. Practical structures have extended at a number of points to confuse my sense of how things used to be. But the purgatorial wing stands clear and unobstructed with its odd exterior brick and concrete fire-

escapable staircase angling up along the side to a little second-story porch that overlooks what's left of the playground. There's enough left to imagine it, recover how it felt, I think. Almost. That potent emptiness of childhood. That contentious ground. I guess some sort of contention was involved. It felt like something was at risk. This angel asking us to set aside our perfect understanding, to consider that it all might be discardable. That one should have to figure out what things are, moment to moment. Rediscover oneself in doubt. Rebuild the picture over and over. How can you get anywhere like that? The mist takes over in that case. Manila paper has its way, imparts its qualities. From up here on the porch—we weren't allowed up here, I think, except for fire drills—I can follow the weedy grass where it used to go, imagine it running under the basketball court and the other additions, a broad expanse of grass clear out to the four-foot chain-link fence, that same old chain-link fence that still surrounds the schoolyard. It remains unsatisfactory. As I've come to understand it. Standing up here on the purgatorial porch and trying to reconstruct the picture and the problem. I remember actually wincing at her approval. Isn't that strange? That I'd achieved it. Found it easy to produce the sort of picture she required. But took no pleasure in it. So you want an ugly, mottled, messy sort of picture, right? Let's see what I can do then. First, ignore what, in my heart, feels like the truth. Then pick the crayons that seem least essential, furthest from the critical idea; that represent in fact erosion, indecision, ambiguity. That compromise the fundamental thought, let all that background, all that brown and orange and yellow fear and desire get mixed up in it. Get the system and the subject all confused. Is this what angels want? I guess I went along. But it remains unsatisfactory. Refuses to resolve. That same old neighborhood out there, the line of cars along the street. A realistic Sunday morning—how do you make any sense of that? Just as it is? Where is the workable idea?

My friend Chuck Watson made a cloud chamber once, he says. When he was a kid in junior high. He had a basement room where he was left alone to pursue such projects as he found described in the pages of *The Boy Engineer* or *Scientific American*. What he remembers is the darkness (and it's hard not to inflect the sense of darkness here—as silly as it sounds, inside the fish tank or the Mason jar or whatever he used—with what I've come to know about the sadness of his childhood) with the flashlight held up to it, all alone down there, a balloon hooked up somehow to be deflated, popped, or something to reduce the pressure suddenly at the critical point inside the jar, the vessel, charged with alcohol-soaked cloth and mounted upside down on a cake pan filled with ice. But all alone down there in the dark with this cold device, his flashlight held up to the side—and having not had much success all afternoon; such things are naturally very delicate, dependent on so many subtle variables. It was a trick to get the angle right, to shine it into the dark inside the jar just right to catch whatever happens, if it happens, let the pressure drop to the dew point or below . . . and then what? What is going on? The rest of the household settled down into the indifferent clatter of dishes, muffled television laughter. So what then? Here's what's remarkable: experience as removed from all that sad, indifferent life as it is possible to be and yet right there within it all the time, invisible till now. The dark in the jar goes cloudy, misty like he's breathed upon the glass, and then a streak, or possibly not, it's hard to tell, you blink, it's gone, but then another, surely, straight down like a strand of cobweb pulled and snapped to show the ghostly ionizing path from space, it had to be from space, a cosmic ray, straight through the sky, the house, the mist inside the jar. I think he must have held his breath. To sense himself impinged upon like this. His cold, somewhat evacuated life brought to a state of such unbearable sensitivity.

Somewhere among my mother's things I've packed away in pale gray cardboard boxes is a picture of my father that I drew when I was five or six. That I remember drawing—not the usual stick schematic but a portrait. As it were. What I intended as a study of his face to get the feeling of it. Something about the wide, thin line of mouth I can remember meaning some-thing. I can remember that. And then, as I was putting things away, to come across it, know exactly what it was and not be able to make any sense of it at all. Like suddenly seeing, and remembering, what things look like to a dog. The mindless clarity. A loose confederation of experimental symbols for the features, gathered signs for nose and mouth and eyes all float-ing on the surface, vague Manila paper surface, of what seemed like a clear idea, a workable idea. I think I thought I had it down. Had got the feeling of him caught in there somehow. I felt his sternness and his kindness were successfully involved. But now—my goodness. What in the world? Each symbol, here again, a world unto itself. Just drifting by and by some accident assembled into something I had feelings for. These deep unal-terable feelings.

All our feelings, I'm convinced, are simply varying propor-tions of desire and fear. Chaotic interaction of the fields. Events pass through or get deflected, scattered, clumped and all so suddenly, surprisingly, it's hard to know what's happening. You do the best you can to get it down, to find a reasonable nota-tion. Something quick and clear to mark it as it passes. Check it off before it's gone. Why did she feel she had to put a stop to that? It could have worked. It might have held together somehow. Why did she lead us out and sit us down and make us reconsider, pause and look to think about it, draw it out, belabor the thing, the moon and stars, the grass, whatever? How much time did she think (do angels think) we have?

SCIENCE FICTIONS
#1

———

Not long ago, I caught the end of some science-channel program having to do with electron microscopy. They were summing up in the presence of the most powerful electron microscope in the world, whose clean and vast and serenely inexpressive rectilinear bulk had TITAN printed on the side and filled the room with a sense of bigness here in principle. Abstracted. A compensatory impulse in there somewhere, I suspected, to establish at the start the fact of size, the big idea. To get the massive physical facts down first, to reaffirm all that before proceeding in the opposite direction. Otherwise, it seemed to me, you might get lost, the physical facts called into question. I mean this thing looks at atoms—in a crystalline array, bright points imponderable as stars. Can't you imagine getting tangled up in the complexity of a machine like that, to the point where you're not so certain where you are within the scrutinizing process—in what surely must consist of layers of systems whispering finer and finer electromagnetic rumors of the truth on up the chain. I can remember back in college coming down with the flu—at my mom's house, in my bed and drifting off into that leading edge of fever, chills, and general loss of personal definition, as it seemed, until such simple understandings of the world as had to do with big and little, mass and masslessness felt strangely insecure, refused my grasp as, on the one hand (in my dreamy state of mind it came to hand), a locomotive felt the same as, on the other, something tiny like a pin, with the confusion given a hard, impossible, sickening, contradictory sort of texture of its own that spread to the other sensory realms and got me out of bed to turn on all the lights, upstairs and down, to no effect. To send my mom away and ask her not to speak. I'd lost my feeling for the world. I knew what things were—just not how it felt to know.

It lasted ten or fifteen minutes and I've never been more frightened. Which, I'm sure, explains the twinge, that little pinprick along my spine, on contemplation of the Titan. Who in the world designs such things? Who gets to know what's going on in there? I want to imagine a guy like that. Who designs electron microscopes—or certain specialized subsystems. Works in Princeton, say, or Boston, up there somewhere with some university program in obscure and complex partnership with West Coast manufacturers. Who lives about an hour's drive away in a nice old house in a nice old rural-feeling neighborhood with his wife of many years, who, though no longer teaching full-time, substitutes in the local schools, is still attractive, smart, and interested in things, is always good with plants and children and their two grown sons and families when they visit. And whose natural, easy grace seems, over the last few years, to have turned more inward somehow. She's let her hair go straight and white or nearly white in a simple bob, what he suspects must be a bob, that he's prepared to approve should it ever come up, which it hasn't really. Isn't that curious? Missed his chance way back there, it would seem. And it would seem it's too late now. What's there to say about it now: "You know,

I've given it some thought . . ." Across the gulf between their stations in the evenings—he in the laptop's glow at the old pine Shaker desk next to the fireplace, she across the room on the couch beneath the big green-shaded floor lamp with a book or turned to watch TV. That's two years probably, fifteen feet of evenings intervening. An impossible distance surely. "What?" she'd say and lift and turn her face, her haloed smile, adjusting for the interval, the shadows, the rotation of the earth, toward him. And then what? Try again? How can you tell if a thing like that makes any sense at such a distance?

He likes driving home each day. The drive itself. From a fairly rigorous, highly organized state of things to a somewhat lower. Somewhat artificial these days, he supposes, yet still genuinely preservative of something once quite close to where our lives emerged for our consideration. I've not spent much time up east but I remember how it feels. My girlfriend, Nancy, who grew up in Massachusetts, Pennsylvania, and Virginia, can remember pretty clearly—all the trees, the maples, birches, oaks and sometimes mighty oaks. A deep and mulchy sort of thatch that's always damp beneath the trees. Jack-in-the-pulpit (now protected), blueberry bushes where it's sandy; where it's wet, skunk cabbage, scum and moss and cattails, stone wall remnants here and there. And sometimes, as you leave the highway in the evenings, little mists you'll find have risen into the slightly warmer air above the creeks and drifted out across the lawns to demonstrate this subtle lower state of things beneath the yard lights and the brighter, colder mercury-vapor lights above the white-fenced pastures, one such pasture, one such mercury-vapor light to mark the corner where he turns and where he's comforted to note, each time it's there, a big gray horse is usually standing.

I imagine he has something like a briefcase—not much in it,

but a bulky-looking briefcase. Not everything can be compressed. There might be journals, special files, reports from engineers, even legal papers—though I shouldn't think he's much involved in that. He is involved in the idea—perhaps not deeply, philosophically. But, over time, habitually. The thought of it seems cumbersome. Of late he feels encumbered. Such an airy, easy house to move around in. The kitchen too, you pass right through, don't think about it. Here's your inside and your outside, light and dark. What's to encumber? Be encumbered? Not the shadows or the mists. The growing old. That's not a thing. It has no mass. It is a quality of things. A sort of field in which things alter and distort. But not so much as to encumber—quite the other way, in fact. Things tend to lighten, drift apart. The briefcase always goes beside the little desk. It's not a genuine Shaker writing desk, but it's old. And very plain. And very purposeful with the briefcase there beside it. What has happened? He allows himself to wonder—once out loud, to give it weight, to see if, uttered, it was marked, stained like a substance to be studied, to be followed, just the question, like a gas as it dispersed. "What?" she called back from the front of the house where she was placing plants in pots. "What?" he returned. So much for that.

It seems so natural that astronomers should develop out of childhoods filled with wonder at the heavens. Farm kids raised where stars are visible. I remember coming across a touching photograph of the young Clyde Tombaugh standing out by some wheat field (what I want to recall as a wheat field) with his spindly homemade telescope as if it were a ribbon-winning sheep or a brand-new piece of farm machinery. Easy as that. Inevitable as that. Where does the young microscopist go to have his picture taken? Hard to say. Does wonder enter in? Does he remember? Maybe something about the nearness in itself.

That it began as simple everyday experience come to hand and brought so close. Then, under scrutiny, disintegrating, held too close to see anymore. Is it the loss that fascinates? You think you're going to nail it down, this piece of stuff, but then it's just too much to hold the thing you thought it was before, so you try again. It is the kind of gaze that tries to find the splinter. You can feel it but you can't get at it somehow. You've no doubt it's there, its presence irrefutable as Rutherford's famous inference of the atom. So what happens?

I suppose he tries to settle down, decides it's how things go, that life attenuates—is that the word? He thinks it is. He thinks he likes the rows of potted flowers she's arranged out on the porch, along the walk. So many colors. Primrose maybe. All the same but different colors. Each in the same little red clay pot. It is incredibly sweet and inexplicably distant, as if somehow at the edge of observability. Like the impossibly brilliant colors of impossibly distant galaxies you've seen in those Hubble photos. You'd think color would be the very first thing to go. It seems so fragile. Accidental. And yet here it is, so sweet and yet so distant.

One night, much later (this, I think, is how it probably ought to go, more like a story), he is up quite late and steps out on the porch. It's cool but pleasant and the mists have drifted in. It hasn't happened lately much, but still, it will when the air is warmer than the water in the streams—or maybe the other way around. It's fifth-grade science, but he really can't remember. And, although it's not his habit, he decides to take a walk. No preparations. He just finds himself by the street where the curbless pavement decomposes into the grass and, looking up and down, the house lights in the mist seem to have drifted in as well. And so it seems a good idea, somehow. Past two or three blocks of tidy, older houses like his own. Some dark already, some still lit with TV light. Around the curve at the end of the block with the black-on-yellow cautionary arrow on a post to warn that here we must accommodate the older cowpath lay of things, not simply barrel on as some have done, as testified by the bent steel posts and barbed wire tangled up against the scraggly oaks that border what was agricultural land at one time, surely, though he's never seen it planted. Now it's just a deeper darkness as he passes. It's so strange—he's not sure what his hands should do. Just let them swing or go in his pockets. Not a choice requiring much consideration, as a rule. This sort of walking, though, is different. Not a thing he usually does. A little wood-railed, two-lane bridge you don't even notice when you're driving. Then a rise toward the white-fenced pasture on the right. Way on the other side the cold, white mercury light that marks the corner. Makes you glad for warmth and simple incandescence. Makes him feel he shouldn't mind to be encumbered. Shouldn't be out here, unused to this. Unpurposeful. Uncertain of his hands, his grasp. Of how he ought to hold himself at all. It's getting chilly. He proceeds along the fence. He likes the fence. Real painted wooden planks and very well maintained. Cold, wet white-painted post-and-rail. He's in the grass, his shoes and trousers getting wet. He really should have worn a jacket. Near the corner, near the light it's all involved in misty glow. He stands awhile and takes his hands out of his pockets. Here we are. He thinks. Decides to think as if it were an established point of interest. As if there were a tour of old microscopists behind him. Here, you see? A paler gray against the dark beyond the cold white glare presents itself. Detaches from its privacy, its unimaginable purposes, and stands some yards away a little sideways, drops and lifts its head and seems to look at him. He steps to the fence and onto the bottom rail, then gets his arm hooked over the top.

How in the world might he explain? We are microscopists, you see—my colleagues here and I . . . the horse is simply looking. Is it strange this horse should still be out in the pasture at this hour? He has no idea. If asked, he could not estimate the strangeness. Find the point upon the chart where two lines cross. He rearranges himself. Secures himself upon the white rail fence. Extends a hand. And it comes over. Just like that. The whole great thing, which sort of thing he has no comprehension of, nor ever will, comes over. Walks right up. And here it is. The great gray head right here within that tiny, careful space belonging only to oneself, within which only things to have or eat or love may generally enter. Nose to hand; then, very slowly, hand to massive side of jaw, along the neck. A little pat. Then somehow getting one leg over the middle rail to brace himself, to free his other arm, to bring both arms up to it, holding there. A flinch, a shudder, deep and soft expulsion of breath. The sound of traffic far away. He is so cold. There's such a volume to its smell and to its breathing. Like a regular shift in atmospheric pressure. Here we are. His hands discover how to place themselves and then he has his cheek against it, finds it's even possible to hold himself, the whole side of his face, against it, keep it there a moment as descends upon him quietly and darkly such a joy and peace as he has never known.

SCIENCE FICTIONS
#2

(for C.W.)

———

So you get somebody crazy enough and rich enough to do this with conviction. Buy the land and bull it through. Hire all the lawyers, pay the necessary tribute, overwhelm the legal difficulties. Form some sort of new municipal zone and cause to come into existence, in the bleakest part of town, the Trinity River Bottoms Homeless Park and Astronomical Observatory. Maybe a hundred acres—no paths or trees or anything, just grass kept like a golf course or a cemetery. Constantly, and more or less invisibly, maintained. And scattered, here and there, across these green one hundred acres, leaving space at the center for the observatory itself, small concrete shelters. All exactly the same. I'm thinking precast-concrete box-culvert sections. Six by six by eight, say, or whatever standard size comes close. You see them on construction sites sometimes—those open-ended concrete boxes. If you think of them as shelter, there's an eloquence. That hard, cold open-endedness. In that we're all just passing through. You know? Essential homelessness, you see. But it's the arrangement that's most critical, I think. It must be beautiful. How can it not be, though—so long as it doesn't get too structured. It should seem a sort of scatter, all those empty concrete boxes on the grass. What's happening here? And at the center like a dream, this great domed building, also concrete, with its heavenly implications.

This has always been a terrible part of town. The hopeless center of West Dallas. Lead-contaminated flat land by the river where the bodies tend to turn up and the streets have names like Fish Trap, Life, and Nomas. This is the area that, according to my old friend Nolan White, who, from the fifties until his murder in the eighties (and whose tales of his grandfather's life under slavery I somehow neglected to record), lived not too far away, across from my father's automobile battery warehouse, where junked batteries were collected for their lead content and hauled straight to the smelter down the road—but anyway, this was the region he remembered, back in the thirties before the levees were completed, as the Bottoms, where respectable people weren't advised to go. But if they did, they should be armed and should not linger after dark.

It never really gets too dark down here at night. It gets opaque. It closes in. The dust and haze and bleary sky-glow from downtown. It is no place for an observatory. They belong on mountaintops, we know. We'll have to force it. And who knows if anyone will even come—it's not so much to offer, is it? Precast-concrete culvert sections. The observatory staffers, of course, get paid—to wear white coats, to try their best to use the telescope and figure out what possible application there might be for such a large and optimistic-looking instrument down here at the very bottom of the world. But as for the homeless, who can say? Perhaps, as the local news gets bored, there is a gradual, intermittent, and uncertain drifting in. Around the edges first. The little concrete—What to call them? Perma-Potties?—spaced among the residential units might serve as an attraction. There's no signage. Various rumors of the most fantastic sort will circulate. The armed security guards are likely to intimidate, though trained to be receptive, helpful, friendly when approached. Who knows how that will work out—otherwise, though, everything will start to go unstable pretty quickly. Without means to filter out the bad intentions, keep it safer than the street. It starts to sound too complicated. But as long as you can see through complication to the basics, it should work—the concrete facts the homeless find themselves addressing every day, but clarified here within this place, admitted to, and purified past all resentment, I am hoping from both sides, at such a silliness, the waste, the presumption. Do it. Simply do it. Let them come and see what happens. Spring and summer, fall and winter. Here's our homelessness at last. Here's what we're dealing with. It's deeper than you think. Can you imagine after a while how it might be, the sounds of maintenance and other practicalities having slipped into the background. Just the natural—what should come to pass for natural—coming and going, ebb and flow of things. Especially at evening. Like a breeze. The sounds of settling down would come across in waves, old feelings somehow at this moment emerging in uninterpretable ways. The calls and sighs and who knows what it means. And all the coughing and the yelling and the opening of containers as the daylight fades and the big dome turns and opens from the garden of the hopeless at the bottom of the world.

SCIENCE FICTIONS

#3

—

Bob Goes to Live Under
Mary Kay's Pink Cadillac

N THE EARLY SEVENTIES, AS THE ARCS OF OUR POSTGRADUATE expectations seemed to be losing loft and conviction and the music seemed to be playing somewhat slower and the need to find a seat before it stopped had occurred to most, although not all, and everyone had already lived with everyone else for a time, it seemed, and the whole idea of domicile and self-reliance made for reluctant conversation—in this sad, departing summer of our lives, my friend the poet Robert Trammell lived for a while with me and my mom. My mom, an old free-thinker herself, enjoyed my arty, pseudobohemian friends, and Bob, perhaps the artiest and most deeply pseudobohemian of us all, fit in quite happily, picking through her rather strange selection of books and watching bad TV in the evenings, though *Kung Fu* was pretty good. We really got into that *Kung Fu* test of enlightenment and reaction time, sometimes well into the night out on the patio, drinking our way toward the true way, snatching pebbles from each other's open hand. It was during this time that Bob—responding, perhaps, to these simple domesticities—conceived that it would be a most amazing and important and poetic thing were he to go and make his home beneath the big pink Cadillac we'd noticed always parked in the drive of the house, not far away, of a wealthy cosmetics manufacturer.

He sort of basked in this idea for a while. We'd joke about it. Marvel at the justice of it—his becoming something like a moral visitation, like gout, the painful consequence of opulence and excess. Or, a little more dramatically, the Phantom of the Opera or the Hunchback of Notre-Dame, the dark imponderable at the center of our loftiest affections. He began to imagine what he'd actually need: a few small tools, the means to siphon from the gas tank (for the camp stove) and the radiator (should there be some workable filtration system—failing that, a means for gathering rainwater or an expansion of the protocol to allow an occasional visit to the faucet or the pool while on those requisite excursions undertaken in the small despairing hours when the world is fast asleep and there is none to watch the slow, precise detaching of himself, the separation of the shadow from the mechanism, something like the soul released to drift across the lawn into the plantings for a while and maybe even into the dreams of she who sleeps above in splendor under fragrant moonlight-colored layers of anti-aging cream).

He would need lightweight, dark-colored, water-repellent clothing. Maybe a jacket for the colder months. A flashlight and a radio. A picture of his Scandinavian girlfriend—in a little oval frame perhaps, with a magnet on the back. A pen, a notebook. Bungee cords and marijuana. He would probably need to consult one of those Chilton automotive guides devoted to that particular year and model. He would have to make a study, as would anyone preparing for an extended stay in some exotic country. As did Dracula, of course, before embarking on his fearful journey west. As did Thoreau, don't you imagine. Take your time and figure it out, devote yourself to the idea, and then, when it's right—you might want to wait for a storm, a terrible night with lightning scattering all across the city, rushing, twisting wind and bending trees and window-rattling thunder all night long—then you go in, in the middle of that, insert yourself as if the moment had developed from within the actual process of the storm.

And there you are. It seems impossible at first. But then you feel around and touch the blackened surfaces, inhale the dark eternity of this, the mix of fluids spilled and burned. The light-ning flashing off wet concrete gives you glimpses of the struc-ture so obscure in its reality, like the history of the underclass, ungraspable except by slow, assimilating stages. Not till dawn do things let up. The tattered clouds withdraw before the pink-and-golden light that, from an upstairs window, shows it's all okay—blown leaves and twigs and a branch or two in the drive but all is well. The pink of the Cadillac has never shown so purely pink before, as if there could be any purity in pink, as if it could be understood as fundamental, even primary, in some way—the blush of passion as experienced or as skillfully applied.

Bob felt there ought to be a point at which his instincts should turn inward. All his cunning with regard to stealth, con-cealment of the evidence—the smoke, the smells, the residue, the groanings in his sleep, those soft, unbidden little noises that emerge on contemplation of the photograph, whose bright, clean, snowy Scandinavian distance stretches out behind her fading smile forever—when all that has fallen away and he no longer needs to care, it is because he's come to inhabit the Cad-illac truly and completely. He has come to understand his place within it. Found the yoga-like positions corresponding to the circumstances, sensed the pallid color of desire as emanating from himself, as percolating from these elemental regions where he rides along, essential to it now, adept at snatching raw materials from the street. Half-eaten meals and bits of clothing if he's lucky. All of life in its disintegrated forms comes back around to him. He's at that deep, regenerative level. At the level of the barnacle, the saint perhaps, the Cadillac infused with him at this point. They reduce toward one another, and inevitably there are compromises—subtle at first but gradually more detectable. Gas mileage suffers—hardly an issue ordinarily, of course, in such a vehicle. But noticeable after a while. A sort of lassitude or something about the steering, about the functioning in general—you can tell when something's changed, a general change, you know. Before you know it, even. An alteration in the basic terms of things. A Cadillac—well, that's a thing to be relied upon to carry certain assumptions. There's a mass and a momentum to appearances—that's one. Conviction overpowers error is another. Doubt is weakness. Life is sweet. And so on. There are smells that come and go. And dreams. And so at last it's taken in and hoisted up. And there is quiet in the bay. Pneumatic power tools fall silent. From within the glass-walled waiting room she watches with her driver till she's summoned. Eyes of four or five blue-uniformed mechanics fix upon her. They withdraw at her approach, then stand around not saying anything. Not getting back to work. A radio somewhere across the shop plays Mexican songs of love and loss. Her own mechanic stands by quietly with a work light and a look of vast apology, as if to say there's nothing he can do. As if, were she not dressed in such a delicate print, her presentation of herself so near the fragile verge of passion, pink and saffron shading into frail translucencies of age, all love and loss as it turns out, he might reach out to take her shoulder, guide her under. But she follows, gazes up with him. A short, soft phrase in Spanish is repeated over and over right behind—they've gathered in. The light's too bright and there is nothing for a while. What should it look like anyway? What should she be expected to find in any case? She's never looked beneath her Cadillac before. She's never listened to Mexican music on the radio. She knows, of course, those mariachi bands that play in restaurants—so exuberant and colorful and festive. Not like this. What is he saying over and over just behind her? Like a prayer. She looks and looks until it strains and starts to darken at the edges. Light draws in to a sort of halo, which surrounds a sort of face. Is that a face? What sort of face is that—so battered and composed? Is this what she's supposed to see? What is he doing under her Cadillac? A couple of the mechanics and a woman from the office have knelt down. Can she emerge from this somehow? She must look awful in this light. Is this a miracle? Is there another car that she can take? Can she be beautiful again?

NAMELESS

——

How can I make this mean what it should? I will insist at least on meaning of some broad, unspecified sort. To get it started. I read somewhere—and I'm sure it came from an exalted source—that the study of the Torah is so virtuous beyond all other virtues, that a gentile, even a gentile, who applies himself brings immeasurable joy to God. So here we go.

My friend the artist Doug MacWithey owned a huge, historic, three-story former Odd Fellows hall in Corsicana, Texas. Though the scale of his work was usually rather small, he was inspired by these immense old spaces, loved, as much as anything, the sense of grand necessity, the fitting out, in this case, of the upper floors—their great high windows looking, from the corner, east and south along the main street—with these massively timbered ten-foot working tables of the kind that might, a hundred years before in similar vast, unheated rooms, have supported ranks of grim industrial sewing machines or something manned, as it were, by ghostly, sad-faced women. And although the big ideas that might have needed ten-foot tables never quite got into gear, and as his work, in fact, reduced to narrowing views of a very narrow field of interest, he required, all the more I think, all that expansiveness for reasons I was unable to appreciate (we had a running joke about the Disney character Goofy carving a toothpick from a tree), or fully appreciate at least, until after his death.

I think such spaces meant to him a kind of endlessness. Historical and physical. Whatever concentrated, pared-away-to-almost-nothing bit of art he did, he wanted to be endless. As if nothingness and endlessness depended on each other. Even some isolated scribble would, in his heart, belong to an endless series endlessly elucidating endless variations on its faint, essential self. And when, as toward the end of his life, a single thought took hold, he'd go with it, he'd crank it out (most times with a little xerographic help) with no intention of ever shutting down until some practicality, like death of course, intruded. This is why he loved the Xerox machine so much, I am convinced—less for the time saved copying patterns than for the endlessness implied. How it suggested art might be cranked out forever automatically, might heap right up to the ceiling, spill from the windows, fill the street with blowing handbills bearing glimpses, advertisements, of the truth. You can't escape it, can't ignore it in a little town like that. All of a sudden here it comes, the blessed truth, right down the middle of the street.

It took a while to get a sense of what he'd left behind. He had a kind of system but it wasn't known to others, and it changed from time to time: the way he'd think about those hundreds of accumulating pages tucked away in plastic folders (he imagined a sort of book); how they referred to one another; to their source, an early-seventeenth-century series of alchemical engravings called "The Seals of the Philosophers," whose 160 enigmatic figures—each assigned to one of the great alchemical worthies, real or mythic; each in that weirdly mechanical allegorical style that seemed to assemble secret knowledge out of parts of the everyday world mixed up and recomposed at random—whose figures he intended to revisit like old research data needing fresh analysis by up-to-date techniques. The hundreds of drawings that emerged (he called them drawings, even the transfers and the pasteups, whether or not a pencil ever got involved—something he resisted, as approaching a kind of "showiness," I think, or even worse an intervention in what ought to be an automatic process), what emerged, though, he had filed away in categories subtle and mysterious and wise beyond our puny understanding. His wife, Karan, who was closest to his thoughts on all of this, had no idea how he'd imagined it should finally come together. It was certain that there was to be a set of 160 numbered "emblems" corresponding to his seventeenth-century model. It was likely, furthermore, that he'd imagined it continuing toward the production of 160 sets of 160. And beyond, the way he would. Why not keep going, he would think. If this is it, and it probably is, just keep on going. And we had another joke—or not a joke but an exemplum having to do with the comedian Richard Pryor, who, in the famous freebasing incident, having set himself ablaze, began to run and, still on fire, conceived that he must not stop, for if he were to stop, he'd be consumed, so there was nothing for it, in his mind, except to keep on running. On and on. Perhaps forever.

So it seemed we had been left with an eternity of images. A beautiful idea. A sort of extrusion, a sort of drawing out forever of the whole idea of meaning. I think he thought he might get under these in a way, these esoteric seventeenth-century re-imaginings of the ordinary world. Like circus posters—see the mystical conflated beast, the self-devouring monster. Just crawl under, get a glimpse of what compels that sort of thing. What forms the impulse that must operate in all of us at vastly lower energies than here, beneath our notice all the time. I think that might be what he was after, what he left us—something like an active principle. The yearning sensitivity to meaning unencumbered, opened up. The empty emblematic gaze.

When he stopped running, when he dropped dead in the middle of the night in Uncertain, Texas—I'm not kidding, in a cabin under a full moon at the edge of Caddo Lake in the nearly nonexistent town of Uncertain, Texas, right out into which, right out into whose dirt streets and whose vagueness and that vague, unsettled dark that comes behind the setting moon, still in her nightgown, Karan ran to scream for help, she who had borne herself through childhood on the phony graveyard mists of British horror films and loved to lock herself away for hours in her family's green-flocked, gold-appointed bathroom to approximate the grandeur of those Hammer production sets and, in her mother's fancy nightgown, practice turning the doorknob slowly; all that practice useless finally; nothing for it when it's real; it has no meaning—but at that point, as he dropped (a pad of notes, his endless notes, there on the table) he had come to terms with what the will to meaning probably looks like by itself. And it reminds me of a gaudy British horror movie I saw many years ago where scientists imagine they have photographed the soul—a startled, skittery faint blue light.

Here's what it looks like: Take an emblem—one of the seventeenth-century images in "The Seals of the Philosophers"— and set his corresponding piece beside it. Here is emblem number 9 from the original engravings. "Calid the Jew, son of Gazichus," it is labeled under the motto that surrounds the circular image. I have no idea if any sort of reality attaches to this guy, but he's important, I assume, so near the Thrice-Great Hermes himself at number 1. It is a complicated image, as most are: three seated lions holding up a great, round table, which, in turn, supports an open book and a flaming brazier or chalice, from which smoke ascends into a smoky, mushroom-cloud-like ring, from out of which the blazing sun appears to rise. Well there you go. It's all in place. For all the mystery, look how heavy and well-founded all that is, as if assembled from a kit. How perfectly balanced under the rules of common grav-ity. How a careful child would stack it. And so clearly upon the actual earth, beneath an actual sky. You'd think such mysteries, such visions, would exist in a sort of visionary space. Would seem to have flickered briefly, faintly and mysteriously into view. But no—in almost every case, they're drawn as grounded in the ordinary world. It seems so clunky and mechanical, our longing. You can see how the engraver must have spent more time—and probably had more pleasure—rendering ground and sky, each weed and clod and pebble, the varieties of clouds. Are we to understand that such things are simply out there? Go for a walk out in the country, you might simply come across it. Secret knowledge all stacked up like something left out in the sandbox.

I remember in the little town of Palmer—south of Dallas, about halfway to Corsicana, where a number of my ghostly, sad-faced, agricultural ancestors are interred—attending funer-als with my father as the ancient aunts and cousins of that era and that region, so obscure to me, began to pass away. It seemed for a while we'd make the trip to Palmer every other month or so to stand awhile outside the little white-frame, turreted, turn-of-the-century church, in that strange emptiness, that glare of not much left out here at all, the crunch of gravel as we circu-lated carefully, my father's clear, anticipatory smile that knew the ones he didn't know had photographs at home of ones he probably did. Then filing in to take our seats. Once—I think maybe it was the first of these—a young man in a well-pressed cowboy shirt stood up to sing, and I thought, Oh crap. It was lovely, though. Whatever it was he sang, it was dead-on; he was incapable of error in that moment, of adornment, affectation, in his beautiful, pearly-buttoned cowboy shirt. You couldn't beat it. From within that dark and graceless little church with all that emptiness surrounding.

But the one I recall most clearly—and I think it was the last—was when the preacher seemed to go off on his own, to talk about heaven. He'd been looking into Ezekiel, I suppose, or Revelation and he wanted, on that summer afternoon with all the cicadas out there chattering away, to get down to it. To describe it in its physical actuality. Now, I am told when it comes to figuring the size of the Heavenly City, there can be some divergence of opinion, amounting to several orders of magnitude, depending on the text and whether Greek or Aramaic, how the units are interpreted, and so forth. But I'm guessing he had taken the more conservative view, deciding, perhaps, the smaller possibility contained the greater promise and appeal to the common working faith. And, as we all seemed interested, I think, he took the liberty, departing for the moment the sad matters at hand—the passing away of generations, our bereavement passing through like that invisible ionization that precedes the flash of lightning that is all we have to hope for— leaving that to point toward something true, eternal yet describable, accessible as what? What to compare it to? The way he spoke about it. It was rather like the first amazed reports of Cowboys Stadium. And not to be despised because of that. You must understand, he said. I think he may have actually said, cicadas humming, people fanning with their programs, you must understand how real it is, how wonderful, right here and now, eternity right here, his arms uplifted, all the windows probably open, the cicadas going crazy.

So, place Doug's version of the seventeenth-century emblem number 9 beside his model, and there's not much cor-
respondence. In his drawing, on the right, a penciled circle
painted solid orange inside, to hold the shape and thought, I
guess, of the original round engraving, and, at left, a few loose
xeroxed lines of text—the title and motto from the original and
some similar lines, encouraging love of God, from somewhere
else—but that's about it. "Calid the Jew, son of Gazichus."
Where is he? Is he approaching? Has he left, with his lions and
table and book and chalice? And all his secrets? This orange
circle is as empty as the parking lot outside that little church in
Palmer, Texas. Are we waiting, then? I think that's the idea.
That we are waiting. This is like an open window. The cicadas
going crazy. I think that's what it was like for him. Imagine
him up there, those great high windows propped wide open
to let the summer air come through. To get a breeze. To keep
from sweating on the paper (usually new, white eleven-by-
twelve-inch sheets or old, browned five-by-seven-inch notebook pages, three-hole-punched to demonstrate provisionality,
that these are only notes and therefore endless). Having to
stand away a little, then lean in to do it quickly, trace the circle with a pencil and a crumpled pie-tin template. Imperfect
struggle of a circle. Stand away and wipe his face. The sounds
outside, distinct, immediate small-town noises. Some cicadas
maybe, mostly trains and pickup trucks and voices. And one
time quite late at night, like three or four, when he would
usually be up working, someone walking down the street all
by himself and singing loudly, as he passed, the silly jingle to
a well-known cat-food commercial—hard to render here of
course, without appropriate notation, but whose chorus, sung
by cats, consisted solely of *meows* reiterated to a happy little
march that seemed intended to continue on and on—*meow,*

meow—with touching mindlessness forever down the street into the dark. But wipe his face and take the paint—orange paint, unmixed, straight from the drugstore or wherever Karan bought it, straight from the common, collective notion of orange paint—and lean in quickly keeping, carefully as a child, within the line to paint it orange, to paint out all that marvelous circus-poster allegory, get back to the blankness of that moment just before. Just hold it there within that ionizing moment as we wait for a flash of meaning—Calid the Jew, Hermes or heaven or whatever—to arrive. To find that potent state of mind before we know what we're imagining exactly.

I can imagine him up there in all that space, with his three-hole punch as at some grim industrial process. All the ghosts of all those nineteenth-century garment workers whispering to him, soft as cicadas. You will never finish, Doug. And he knows that. Of course he knows. And that's the deal. And yet they hang around and whisper all the same.

———

SO, WHAT IS TORAH study anyway? I doubt it's much like Bible study class when I was a kid—which seemed straightforward. Mostly having to do with learning the names and order of the books. The study of Torah I imagine altogether more demanding. To be so virtuous. Requiring ingenuity and rigor. I imagine it insists on meaning immanent throughout, at every level. Meaning, not just information, as itself a sort of saturating mystery.

———

IN 1884, IN CORSICANA, down the street from the Odd Fellows hall, which wasn't built yet, there occurred a strange and terrible event. A lone performer came to town. And though some

129 Calid the Jew, son of Gazichus

The creator's magistery is derived from adoration of God, not from

your strength.

You seek the greatest mysteries of our magistery?

By your own labour alone you seek in vain.

However if you seek by pouring out your prayers to God.

The chosen task will have a pleasing end.

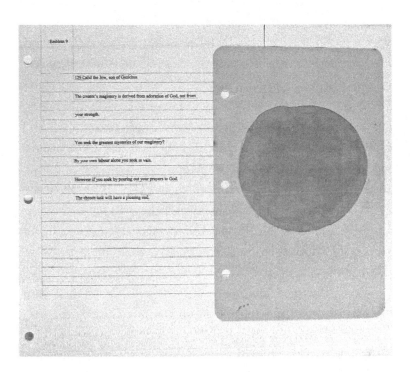

versions of the story (there's a file in the local history room
of the Corsicana Public Library) place him there as an attraction for the opening of a dry goods store or something, most
just have him showing up: a lone, itinerant, Jewish rope walker
with a wooden leg shows up to stretch a rope across a major
intersection from one building to another at a height of twenty
or thirty feet, his peg leg notched to receive the rope; and,
bearing (inexplicably—why in the world?) upon his back a
large, iron cookstove, tries to cross but, halfway over, falls and,
crushed by the stove, expires either there in the street, according to some accounts, or later, according to others, in a hotel
room, but in either case refusing to disclose his name or any
information whatsoever about himself beyond his Jewishness,
attended, in the absence of a rabbi, by a local Jewish merchant
who assists him in reciting, in good Hebrew, prayers for the
dying.

After Doug died, and his studio was photographed, its contents gathered, cataloged, and a good many of them organized
and framed for a really beautiful posthumous show (Can I just
say that without getting all cranked up, all theoretical; without
reference to first principles and going on and on about the clar-
ifying doubt and risk of emptiness that comes to modern art?
Can I just say, Oh crap how beautiful it was?), and all, with
Karan's help, conceived, curated, mounted by Doug's great old
friend the critic Charles Dee Mitchell, at the MacKinney Avenue Contemporary—after that, and after the silence after that,
I think we all calm down a bit and start to come to terms with
things: the loss, the practicalities. The Odd Fellows hall is sold
to a bright young artist friend of Nancy's. And pretty soon
he's got this sort of atelier going—weavers, painters, sculptors
coming down from Dallas, renting space, a communal kitchen.
Ground-floor woodshop. Nancy rents the whole third floor. At

last a place removed from practical constraints where she can set her giant canvases like sails. I come to visit when I can. Her bright young artist friend comes and goes, as do the others. In the mornings it's just me and Nancy usually, making coffee in the kitchen on the second floor. Doug's kitchen. Karan's kitchen. Coffee and doughnuts in what used to be Doug's studio, windows open, propped with two-by-fours, the sounds of trains and voices. And this little stapled pamphlet Nancy's artist friend picked up from the visitors' center. *Walking Tour of Historic Downtown Corsicana.* On page 4, the tale of the wandering Jewish rope walker. Good Lord, Nancy, listen to this.

———

AT DUSK, IF NO ONE'S down there working, I'll descend to the second floor and stand for a while in the southeast corner, where Doug usually spent his time. With windows open on two sides. There is a Main Street, but the real main street is Beaton Street, which runs along the east side of the building. From the south side's east-most window—right behind Doug as he worked—you get the best view straight down Beaton. If it weren't for the trees, not here of course in 1884, you'd see to the Collin Street intersection, which the rope walker tried to cross. From the southeast corner at Collin and Beaton to the northwest, I believe. Doug, at his table, would have been facing away. But were the windows open, as they probably would have been, he would have turned at the sudden silence, then the cries. What had he missed? A vision, surely. Nothing real. But something meaningful, I think. I have decided.

———

THERE'S A PHOTO WITH the article in the pamphlet showing the tombstone marked "Rope Walker" in the Jewish cemetery. Just

a simple round-topped slab. The letters a little too far apart, too near the edge on either side, as if these words were awkward, difficult somehow. I need to see if it's still there. And ask around to see what people think about it. If they think about it. How could they not? Even after so many years. I mean, my God, a cast-iron stove. Right out in the middle of the street, in the afternoon. A peg-legged Jew with a big iron stove strapped to his back, way up in the air. As clear as anything. An ordinary day, and then this happens. What can it mean?

It is suggested we go talk to Marie at the sandwich shop—or, actually, Sandwich Shoppe. She's lived here all her life and loves to talk. Our bright young artist friend has been here only a few months and already he knows everyone. Her sandwiches are pretty good, he says.

I get a Reuben, which, in fact, is pretty good. Whatever Nancy gets is pretty good as well. A pretty good little sandwich shop. An elderly couple sit at a table by the window, holding hands. They haven't got their order yet. At first I think they're saying grace, but they're just holding hands, four hands across the table by the window. She appears somehow bewildered. Nancy thinks that may be how she is and why he holds her hands. They're in between. They'll get their order in a minute but right now he holds her hands. How sad and hopeful. Now it's drizzling. I forgot to bring my jacket. Pretty soon it's time to pay and ask the question. Maybe this will be a children's book. Where the rabbit, say, is on a quest and has to go from place to place and ask whomever he meets—the bear, the lizard, the crow, and so forth—if he's seen what the rabbit is searching for; and each one sends him on until at last he's back where he started and whatever he was looking for was right there all the time. Or else it is way out there somewhere and it's not what he expected. You should go see Babbette Samuels, says Marie.

Babbette is old but she can tell you all about it. I had hoped Marie, who must be in her sixties, might have stories of her own, or might, at least, express some interest in the question. She gets going on more recent local history though. Did we know at one time there were five movie theaters here? We did not. Nice ones too, she says. And then she names them. It appears it's going to be a wet, gray day. We'll stop by the visitors' center next. And then the cemetery.

All the shelves and tables and displays at the visitors' center have been crammed into one room of the little early-twentieth-century railroad building. They're remodeling. Who is there? inquire two ladies from within the little room, beyond the bookshelves. We are visitors. Of course. We are remodeling. I see. I get another of the *Historic Downtown* pamphlets, a map of the county, and directions to the Jewish cemetery. Babbette Samuels, they agree, is the authority on matters such as these. But it turns out she's had a fall and is recovering in a local nursing home.

I can't recall ever having seen old tombstones laid to rest like this. Quite a few of them here in this older part of the Corsicana Hebrew Cemetery. Simple nineteenth-century, arch-topped slabs that—to protect from further breakage or theft, I guess—have been laid flat, embedded in concrete, which appears to have been poured out on the spot. It has the look of an emergency operation. Doug would have loved it. The necessity of it. A diagram of how things fade away. Shovel out a big, more or less rectangular patch of dirt, pour in the concrete, drop the slab, and press it flat. Then stand away and wipe your face. Then let it set. And let the edges, where it thins, begin to crumble. Let the moment of attention pass away. Let no one think too much about it. Here is something pared away to almost nothing—just those two words strung so awkwardly, so strained across the marble, which is framed by even less. The even less, the sad gray concrete, crumbling out to nothing at all at the edge where the mowers or the weed trimmers tend to dig up under into the dirt so it gets muddy all around.

———

WHAT DO YOU THINK could have been seen? Was there a moment, as he fell, when he just hung there? To a child, say, something dangled in the mind. Held in that strange consolidation like an allegorical figure in some Brueghel painting. Goodness, there's your emblem. There's your sudden flash of meaning out of nowhere. And preceding this, a blankness or an emptiness somehow? The sun too bright? A loss of clarity or something as that subtle little shiver in the wire goes wrong and everyone can feel it in their hearts. The children all shut up at once. And there it goes. It all just goes before you know it. Way up there, the whole thing—Jew and stove and balance bar and peg leg kicking out—all up in the air, an object never seen before, a sort of vision for a moment in the buoyant afternoon.

— —

WHAT IS THE MEANING of the stove?

It's hard to say. Just something clumsy and ridiculous to carry. Like a pig or a piano. Though a stove, it's true, was carried once by the great Blondin in 1859 to the very center of a rope above Niagara Falls in order to cook an omelet, which he lowered to the audience on a tourist boat, the *Maid of the Mist*, below. That was a lightweight prop, of course, to make a joke: It smokes, you see? A stove! He camps above the torrent! There's no wit, no cunning here, however. This is not to be explained that way. It's like the kitchen sink. It represents the last thing you would choose. The heavy randomness, the tragedy

of things, of all our sufferings and comforts and desires, against
the perfect thin extension of the rope.

———

AND THERE'S THE WOODEN LEG? The rope itself?

The peg leg is self-knowledge. And the rope is aspiration—
endless, abstract, without substance. It's that endlessness for
nothingness. You see?

———

TOO MANY NURSING HOMES out here. I didn't listen very carefully.
Didn't really think we'd try to look her up, but here we are. I
think. I think we've got it this time. Mainly just to say we followed through, I guess. And who can tell what wisdom waits
down bright and cheery, floral-papered halls. Such long halls.
So many nonsequential numbers. It's a test. If we can pass
through this okay, we have a chance. Her door's ajar. The room
is dark. She's not there, someone says. A woman—not a member of the staff, I believe, just someone being helpful. As if
anyone might know where Babbette is at any moment. One
just knows. The word goes out. She's in the beauty salon. She
should be almost done. She points the way.

And sure enough, she's just about ready. Whichever one of
three or four nearly identical, perfectly coiffed white-haired
ladies cycling through in phase she is. Of course we'll find out
in a minute. We will ask for her and introduce ourselves and
she'll come forward bright and eager to engage on any subject
we might like, though she suspects it is the rope walker as, it
seems, it usually is. And we'll feel silly to admit it. People always want to know about the rope walker, says Babbette, back
in whose room we'll sit and talk, and I will do my best to draw
some natural, darker, broader meaning out of this without suc-

cess. She is so clear and smart and open and pragmatic. She is secretary-treasurer of the cemetery board. At eighty-five, she gets it done. She is responsible for the simple replacement headstone I neglected to describe—above the old embedded slab, a blocky, light gray stone with the date of death as well as the profession cleanly cut and perfectly centered. It's all over, one infers. We are content. It's just a story, she will tell us. People did crazy things like that back then. That's all. But in that moment as we're standing in the door to the beauty salon confronting three or four—I wish I could remember—pretty much identical radiantly white-coiffed ladies gazing back at us so hopefully it seems, all finished up, all ready to go, complete, all equal paths to mysteries of their own, it's as if here we have a choice. Which allegorical white-haired lady shall we pick? Before we speak we must decide, and if we're wrong, what then?

———

DO YOU KNOW THE PAINTING Landscape with the Fall of Icarus, thought for years to be by Pieter Brueghel, but now believed by some to be an early copy? It is a picture of the fruitful, functional sixteenth-century European world as viewed from an eminence above a slightly dizzy slope of farmer's field and pasture falling away to a vast blue harbor whose departing merchant ships sail calmly out past luminous cities in the distance. In the foreground, just beneath our point of view, a tidy red-bloused plowman guides the plow downhill behind his slow plow-colored horse. Below, a shepherd, with his dog at heel, his flock dispersed close by, leans on his staff and gazes somewhat blankly up at nothing visible to us. While down on the rocky shore an angler casts his line. It's all suffused in brilliant sunset. Why not sunrise, I can't say—the art historians seem quite certain. And I suppose, at least in my pallid reproduction, there's a certain weary pallor to the glow. The horse looks tired. So that would mean—to take these things perhaps more seriously than is useful—that poor Icarus, whose tiny thrashing legs are disappearing way out there, beyond the angler, in the bay, would have been falling, if one estimates an apogee at noon, for half a day. Or, who knows, maybe even longer. Maybe centuries—the qualities of atmosphere and gravity and grief were not well known. In any case no one is paying much attention. Look how pliant and obedient all the functions of the earth. The soil folds gently under the plow like pleats of cloth in the plowman's cloak. Auspicious outward-blowing breezes fill the sails of the departing ships. The sheep constrain their browsing, and the angler has a bite. Is it just me, or is there almost always something a little uneasy in Brueghel's pictures of the peasant life? (Here too—no one disputes that, if a copy, it's a good one.) It's the thoughtless, common life. Such life, you'd think, would run together, get averaged out, get lost in browns and grays. What can it mean to bring all that to an almost religious point of clarity? Benightedness itself receives its color and its gesture and its place. There's no ennobling going on, or not exactly, but there is a sort of charge—it could all burst into a Bosch at any moment. It's the thoughtlessness that's clarified. Intensified to a point where you feel like anything can happen.

Let's imagine that Brueghel painted Doug MacWithey. Like the plowman, in the foreground, leaning toward us, working away, while out the second-story window right behind him, in the distance, unaccountable events from long ago are taking place. It makes no sense. And he's oblivious. Pasting something down, I think, and bending so far over the table that all we see is the top of his head, the hump of T-shirt that, historically, was black but here is red like the plowman's blouse. A red for emphasis. To hold him in that moment, to that spot. Late afternoon comes in behind and casts him into his own shadow, so whatever he is working on is dark; his face is dark. Our eye slips past him out the window into the glare, the ambiguity. Out to where the very tiniest brush is needed to show anything. If anything is possible. Way in the distance where the masters of the Torah, if I understand correctly, look for meaning. To catch the whipping of the rope, the glint of balance bar, the strange suspended flailing of it all to show us something we have never seen before. That we had no idea was anywhere except, perhaps, in dreams.

ON WATCHING THE KEN BURNS AND DAYTON DUNCAN DOCUMENTARY ABOUT LEWIS AND CLARK ON PBS

———

'M NOT PAYING CLOSE ATTENTION, JUST FLOATING ALONG WITH them out to the end of everything and back. And at some point I blink to realize they're using photographs, old photographs, as old as they could find, I guess, along with maps and paintings, to confer a photographic actuality on events predating photography by forty years or so. It hardly matters. The photographic actuality of one old Indian seems to stand, quite naturally, for all. Such people lived along the shore of the Missouri in those days. And would have photographed, leapt into actuality, as easily as this old Indian here. There seems to be a certain pleading for reality, a sense of doubt or loss to be addressed. Look how the camera scans these stationary objects—portraits, landscapes—like the eyes of someone wakened from a coma. Sitting up and gazing round to take in not so much the things as the reality of things. The slow, interrogating zoom into the famous painting of Lewis as some stern Shoshone warrior might regard it, first presented with such a thing: Is this a man? What does he have to say to me? How can I know that he is real? You hear the wind across the prairie, through the scrub along the river, as you lean in to examine Lewis's firm yet somehow sad and delicate features. Sad and delicate, of course, is Ken Burns's style. (The same harmonica, so to speak, is always playing.) But I think never so appropriately, expressively, as here. They're on their way to the ends of the earth and it seems natural, fundamental, that the brave, despondent Meriwether Lewis should be leading, and his sadness seem to trail behind like smoke. Not just regret on taking leave of the familiar, resignation to the dangers, to the fatal possibilities. But a deeper sense of going away. Not like at sea, where you're consigned, at once, to placelessness and know, somehow, to gather yourself to yourself for the duration. But to have no destination in a way; to have to pass by destinations all about you, all the clearly promising places along the way where the heart might rest, to come to the place where destinations come to an end. There must have been a different kind of trepidation here, I think. A different kind of risk and doubt. Though not to contemplate— except for Lewis, indirectly maybe, when those dark depressions found him at a loss in every sense and the journal entries come to a stop and nothing moves him but his duty. And these sunsets. What's the deal with all these fading crimson skies whenever the camera brings us back to the present flow of things, the river and the prairie and the mountains as we drift along like not-quite-sleepy children at the surface of some bedtime story, gazing out the window at the evening. Always evening. All that red and gold and shadow on the prairie makes us sad. For what? I wonder. History maybe? Simply that? That seems to be what Burns is good at. Baseball. Civil War. Whatever. It's all out there on the prairie as the sun is going down. Or do we sense in Lewis's dark predisposition what, in us as well, might find itself released, expanded out into those lower-pressure regions where our presence seems unstable and evaporative and difficult to locate with precision.

LOVE IN SPACE

———

WHEN I WAS SEVEN, I IMAGINED I ENJOYED A SPECIAL UNderstanding with regard to outer space. Much like the cowboy's for the prairie or the sailor's for the sea. What was I thinking? I was seven—I remember actually thinking, "I am seven" as I'm standing on the sidewalk near my house one time. I'm looking down and it's the usual sort of concrete sidewalk, scored in sections, each one framed by smoother troweling at the edges, gritty surface. Somewhere, probably, a handprint or the name of someone lucky enough—who knew how many years before—to see the workmen leave and take a chance. And I imagine it was summer, yellow grass along the walk on either side and in the cracks, and I'm just standing there and thinking, "I am seven." I know nothing at that age. I do not know the names of the states. No sense of distances between the most familiar destinations. What is honor, death, or anything. And yet right there in the blazing Texas afternoon, I know that I am seven and I also know the deep and inexplicable, cold and breathless joy of space. How can this be?

There seem to have been, as I think back—and in our hearts there may still be—two kinds of space. The horizontal kind that, back then, came so easily to mind—somehow more gradual and receptive to the horizontal (which is to say the fundamental, thoughtless) imagination. Which is to say, of course, my own. The kind of space required, or presupposed, by the horizontal spaceships that Buck Rogers and Flash Gordon and Commando Cody flew—the ones that had to sputter along the ground for a couple of feet before ascending through the clouds into that odd, residual mistiness that gave the vacuum structure to support all that adventure, I suppose. This was the kind of outer space those coin-operated rocket rides addressed outside the five-and-dime or the grocery store. I loved the one at the little strip of stores a block or so from where we lived. I sensed the silliness but loved the small red button on the otherwise functionless joystick. That the coin drop didn't activate, but only armed the system, gave you access. And then time for the embarrassment to steam away and leave you with a moment to allow the possibility to gather, to extend beyond the idiotic mechanism out across the parking lot and the neighborhood and past all the familiar destinations and the indeterminate intervals between them to a point where you might leave your meager everyday experience behind. But all you got, and all you needed, after all, was that initial lurch. The back-and-forth that followed simply had to be endured. What was important was that sudden thrusting forward that you had to get yourself all set for. Tensed to feel it shove you like a bully in the back. You had to wait. Let passersby pass by and pity you your dimelessness, the pretense; let them go, the ones with rattly metal grocery carts departing with their own kids turned to look. Don't look at them—they pass from under the awning into the light and heat, now craning around. The little ones too, in the folding seat all hot and squinty, folded in among the paper sacks. Don't even think about them. Wait. There needs to be a clear space. Then you hit it. Hit the button. Then a sort of double lurch, to be precise, a double take as if accounting for the disbelief, a nudge as the gears engage and then the big one snaps you back and, for a second, less than a second, though in principle an indeterminate interval, you're gone.

The other kind of space was vertical and difficult and strange. And I'll get to it. But I really need to slip in here to get back to the sidewalk for a minute, check my grounding as it were. (And as I tend to do, apparently—in an earlier piece on baseball I returned to a childhood site to check the scribblings in the concrete.) I am told that concrete never stops consolidating, keeps on getting harder year after year for maybe centuries. I hope that's true. I like to think that concrete is receptive to events—beyond the way it seems to beg to get marked up. It is the fundamental artificial surface, reproducing ground with none of ground's uncertainties. Events embed and hold their place and harden into something to get back to later, maybe. So I try to. So I did the other day. Drove back to that little postwar neighborhood and parked there on the street right next to the sidewalk, which was just as I describe. Dry yellow grass on either side and in the cracks. I should explain that I've never lived very far from anywhere else I've lived. Just driving around, it's like I'm always passing through this sort of vague and rather poorly maintained theme park. Which I guess sounds pretty sad, except I'm very fond of theme parks. All the better if they're fading and the structure of the make-believe shows through. No one's around. I take some pictures of the houses and the sidewalk, which is buckled here and there a little more than I recall but otherwise is still the same. The time of day seems right as well—the sun quite high, the glare and heat that must have fixed that moment, overexposed it into the concrete surface like those shadows at Hiroshima—less visible and less terrible here of course, but no less mortal. This is the place where I was seven in a blaze of natural light. I do my best to hold the camera out away from me and point it straight down. This particular uncracked section feels right. I was walking home, about to turn the corner when I stopped. I'm pretty sure I stopped and looked down at the sidewalk and it caught me. It occurred to me. The fact of me, I think, that just came out like that. Expressed itself that way. Now here I am again and everything's the same. So, later on that afternoon I've got my camera under the magnifying lens above my desk. I'm paging through—a shot of the neighborhood to the west. There's Mr. Saunders's house, the sidewalk, and the street. A shot of sidewalk at an angle. And another at a slightly different angle. Then the one I tried to shoot straight on. I didn't quite get all of it—a strip of yellow grass and a dirty tennis shoe at the bottom. Hit the zoom a couple of times and there it is—just sidewalk. Simple. Like the memory. Why would memory want to hold a thing so simple? What was I *looking* at? Or where had I found myself that I would stop right there, look down, and think that thought? My little camera is kind of old so you have to look straight into the view screen to get full illumination. Angle the screen too far one way and it goes white, too far the other— which is to say away from you—and it goes dark. Not all of a sudden, of course (bear with me here), but gradually, so if you're sitting at your desk and you've put your camera down in front of you with the screen still on, you've got a certain angle—and remember it's that shot of the sidewalk surface zoomed in slightly so it's pretty much the view you'd get if you were three and a half or four feet tall and, being a child who tended to look at things straight on, extremely sensitive to everything, the texture of the concrete and the tiny brilliant particles of pure white scattered all throughout the mix—but anyway, the point is, glancing at the camera at that angle before the power-saver feature shuts it off, you see the darkened shot of the sidewalk, for an instant, as a view of something altogether different. Even opposite in a sense. And it's amazing. It's a glimpse of outer space. As true, as subtle and deep as any shot of space I've ever seen. Those bright and faint and fainter chalky specks just floating over the dark, eternal emptiness like stars.

By vertical space, I mean the kind of space achieved by going straight up. Straight away, without transition or translation. From a point upon the surface to no surface at all. No place for superficial thoughts and sentiments to operate, for horizontal-propagating feelings to occur except, perhaps, as a sort of forced theatricality. Remembered signs and gestures. I would watch *Tom Corbett, Space Cadet* and sense this dark constraint I didn't get from *Space Patrol*, whose graceful, horizontal spaceships you could stroll through like a ranch house, where the latitude of human possibility was generous as well, between the hero and the idiotic sidekick. As if life were understood to have spread out, as it always has, not up, into the distant future. On *Tom Corbett*, life made sorties into space. Straight up. A very narrow passage that required the clearest possible expression of intention and direction. I still have somewhere my old Tom Corbett lunch box, which I don't remember using very much. It made me sad, somehow. A nice blue metal lunch box with exhortatory graphics—lots of spaceships, space, and space cadets posed rocketlike, legs wide like fins, belts grasped with winglike elbows out. I don't know why it saddened me. The space cadets so perfectly straight up in all respects. The sky dead black. The gentle sound wax paper made as I unwrapped my tuna sandwich.

I would vacillate—not thoughtfully of course, not analyti-

cally, but inwardly, emotionally—between *Tom Corbett, Space Cadet* and *Space Patrol*. Between those ways of thinking or imagining. I probably still do. How is it best to get to space? To understand it? Stand on the sidewalk on a hot day. Think about it from the simplest point of view. Consider your age. The joy. The emptiness. In David Clary's *Rocket Man*, a photograph from 1929 shows Robert Goddard, the famous rocket pioneer, along with four of his assistants, posed by the wreckage of a fairly large experiment. They all look pretty happy (even Dr. Goddard smiles) lined up in the scorched grass, standing over the remains, a jumble of twisted tubes and sheet metal that looks nothing like a rocket anymore. And all a little less than two hundred feet from where they touched it off. You have to wonder what's the deal. Two hundred feet. It's been two years since Lindbergh's crossing of the Atlantic. What's to celebrate? What had this rocket done? Where had it been? To bring back something worth a picture, getting everyone lined up out there like that in the empty field. I'd like to suggest it had, in principle, been to space. Or been toward space. In fact it hadn't even gone straight up—went sideways, finally falling to this point where it exploded, frightening everyone for miles around apparently. Which seems to be important—that this perpendicular thinking ought, in principle, to frighten people, bring out the police and the news reporters, which it did, right after the photograph was taken. That it ought to be so difficult and strange. It's just mechanics. What's so hard? Here's aviation—horizontal aviation—soaring into a kind of pure, romantic moment. Breaking records. Glorious posters. What's the problem? Just the angle? Have a look sometime online at the National Archives footage of Goddard's tests. It's crazy. Everything blows up. And sad, the way the seasons come and go. Look—

now there's snow on the rutted ground. And how the sky remains this hazy, overexposed, impenetrable white. It's all so painful, forced, unlikely—as if up against some deep, unstated protocol—that just this much, this wreckage in a field, is worth a little celebration. Not so much, I think, for getting off the ground as for sustaining the intention to escape it altogether long enough to fall out here in an empty field as if from heaven.

I imagine Goddard's neighbors were as sensitive to all this sort of thing as to the weather. I imagine most of them up there near Auburn, Massachusetts, lived on farms and had a farmer's sense of earth and sky and how things go between them. I should think they might have been on edge already. Then a louder one. And longer probably. Long enough, at two in the afternoon, to bring a halt to preparations in the kitchen. Walking over to the screen door, brushing little clouds of flour from her hands against her apron. It is going to the moon this time, perhaps. The clouds drift through the screen, disperse into the yard. A soft explosion in the distance. What in the world must they have thought about all that? How strange, how intimate to have it going on so close to home. As if whatever he was trying for were not so far away. The moon, whatever, as a child might think about it.

———

MY UNDERSTANDING OF OUTER SPACE when I was seven probably had to do with openness more than emptiness. The latter held unthinkable possibilities. The former, something else. I'm not sure what. Whatever it was that little rocket ride was pointed toward, I guess. A place from which the world you know has been essentially removed. Where it remains implied, however. Which is to say where there remains a sense of place. So, horizontal in that sense. And maybe, somehow, amniotic. If, at seven, one were not so far removed from one's beginnings that that darkness might not cast a shadow still.

When Mickey Rooney, in an episode of his 1950s TV show, imagined he and his idiotic sidekick had successfully flown to the moon in their homemade rocket, whereas actually having landed only a couple of miles away in a farmer's field, I was less interested in the comedy than the strained but undiscouraged capability of our belief, of my belief, in his. It is the middle of the afternoon. And here they are on the moon. And there is grass. And sky. And ordinary air, which lets them take their helmets off. And a cow. Just standing out there by itself. A dairy cow, I think. And this is pretty funny when the guys decide it has to be a moon creature of some sort. But right before it gets so goofy, there's a moment with them standing in their space suits on the surface of the ordinary world, two miles from home, among such clear and natural evidence of the world that it appears in a child's first drawings of it—grass and sky and cow—and yet they're seeing it as alien and strange. Who could have known the moon would be like this? Perhaps they've been knocked silly by the landing—nose first; surely they're affected. But I loved it. Kept the memory all my life. The clearest possible distinction—close and distant—penetrated, idiotically, sure, like a drumhead by a clown, but still. Exactly like in Renaissance and ancient comic theater, where identities seem so fragile, arbitrary, trading places all the time. The earth. The moon. Well, who can blame them? It's an easy mistake to make and, after all, no harm is done. It all works out. Except I'd like to change it up. Have Mickey and Freddie (that's the idiotic sidekick) come to terms with what's occurred, their situation and its irreversibility, the curious yet reassuring symmetries— how each world, for example, calls the other one the "moon."

And then the loneliness and sadness that these symmetries evoke. How they assimilate eventually, sometimes waking next to their moon wives in the middle of the night and wondering if their families ever gave up looking for them, might be looking still and sometimes, gazing at the moon, be gazing toward them and not know it. How the light from home shines brightly on the lunar crops and open fields and how the eyes of children here—so nearly human, easily mistaken, so heartbreakingly mistakable for human—widen, brighten at the telling of the story and the bringing out of the space suits every year or so to show them (how their wives will smile and stand away a little). How the myth persists in spite of certain arguments. And how it seems to matter less and less with the passing years, the literal truth against the deeper understanding that accumulates like dust, the kind of dust they used to think the moon was covered with, as fine as sifted flour.

I suspect there is no loneliness in vertical space. No room, as it were, to translate those expansive, horizontal sorts of feelings. Or at least not very much. You'd get this fairly low-grade emotional agitation on *Tom Corbett* now and then, but it was usually expended within those very narrow confines—mostly technical or interpersonal stuff between the more or less identical male cadets. There was no idiotic sidekick (till much later) to diffract or magnify such moments, act upon our sympathies for foolishness as standing for all foolishness. Nor any but the briefest female presence. Human feelings seemed to echo off the curved, metallic rocket-ship interior, bounce around, and cancel out. Not that I sat around and analyzed all this, of course. I'm seven. But I felt it. Something about it. And so strongly that the feeling hangs around, recurs at odd times like those feelings you get when passing on the street some older lady whose perfume trails ghosts behind her, thoughts and longings—always longings for some reason—you'd forgotten from some region of your past that's inaccessible except by such emotional indirection, like a spoor too faint to follow or you follow and it overloads and deadens and you lose it altogether, but which held for just that instant seems to present a garbled rush of so much ancient sentimental information you can't possibly understand it, only feel it, like some complicated waveform it would take a mathematician to untangle. It's like that. And so without the mathematics, one must do the best one can.

I can remember my position on the floor in front of the TV as I watched *Tom Corbett, Space Cadet*. A foot or two away in a sort of crouch. A sense of peering into it. It was serious. Less dramatic, less elaborate, I suppose, than *Space Patrol*. But I would fasten on that seriousness. The clangy sound effects of verticality—they must have used a cast-aluminum pressure cooker like my mom's to make the sounds of hatches opening and closing. Lots of hatches. Ladders. Everything so strenuous. The blastoff most of all. Poor Tom would writhe beneath the forces of ascent. Why *wouldn't* I crouch? I didn't know how this would go. To have to suffer just to leave the ground like that. That's one of those things that could affect you for a while. In bed at night to try to feel it for yourself—what kind of dark would cause discomfort risen into? Not this kind. This horizontal kind that lies upon my bed and fills the room. That has the quality of thoughtfulness and stillness that fills all the little apprehensive darknesses you learn to pay attention to. Don't put your hand up under there, you think, but then you do and there's that moment when the dark you think is probably inside you (as I say, you're not so far from your beginnings) rushes forth and you jerk back and hold your hand though you're not injured in the slightest. You've not formed the hard distinctions yet. And so you're very sensitive. You scrunch your eyes and throw your arms out sideways on the bed and think about it. Try to imagine taking off to outer space and it's like nothing. There's no writhing. What Tom Corbett rises into must be different. You can tell. How, given the impulse, maybe a little shove for emphasis, you'd lift into it easily. Even the air, at last, could peel away and leave the dark like carbon paper (Who remembers carbon paper? I knew carbon paper), all the information pressed into it invisible yet recoverable, implicit. So, in fact, you're losing nothing. There's no struggle.

———

I MUST BRING UP Dayton Miller. He's come up before in other things I've written. His experimental struggles against the Michelson-Morley results, against the emptiness of space and relativity. I want to get back to him in the 1920s when he's spending all that time up on Mount Wilson with his giant interferometer enclosed in a fragile tentlike structure it was hoped would be like a screened porch to the cosmological breeze, which is to say permit detection of the "luminiferous ether"— that imponderably subtle substance many still believed (notwithstanding the Michelson-Morley results and special relativity) must pervade all space with means for light to propagate and common sense to keep our amniotic understanding of the emptiness in place. It would take months to bring it out. To sift, develop all the data to extract this thoughtless, precious, dare I say it horizontal understanding out of nothing, out of emptiness itself—to find, in the clearest, most objective way, the emptiness configured to receive our simplest longings. What are the odds? It would assume the essential vacancy of space to be an immanent, expressible, and absolute condition, present everywhere among us and within us, through which we are always passing and to which we have forever been resigned. And into which the subtle light of this device is introduced as into a stillness, as a candle thought to flicker in the presence of a ghost. He'd have to gaze at it while turning it, recording it, for months—the light, a confluence of two beams producing a pattern known as "interference fringes," which discovered, upon analysis, to have shifted, to have flickered, in a regular and statistically meaningful sense, would mean that one or the other converging beam of light was being retarded, like a boat turned into the current, as the device was turned as the earth moved through the (therefore not quite) emptiness of space. As if the emptiness were a comprehensible thing, like air or water.

I must wonder if it's meaningful to wonder how it felt. I mean it's such a curious physical situation. A bucolic slope of ground up there on the mountain, pines or firs, what look like cedars maybe, wooden-posted wire fence in the foreground with a small steel, wire-strung gate across a worn path I suppose he would have used. No cows. You look for one. There ought to be a cow. To go with the grass and trees and pale, impenetrable sky. The wood-frame structure housing the instrument might serve as well for storing hay or feed. It has that practical, perfunctory agricultural sort of look. Or, in the photograph in William Fickinger's biography, which shows the white-cloth insulating covering in place, like a tent revival setting up—that kind of sentiment quite naturally arising from the simple facts apparent here, that yearning to detect the Spirit passing like a breeze, a smell of rain. He'd had the whole thing hauled up here. In a sense, the whole accumulated mass of forty years' experiment hauled up from university basements where they'd come to the conclusion that the failure to obtain a clear result was best accounted for by ground-level disturbances—involving local mass as well as that of the earth itself—which ought to be reduced, they reasoned, at greater altitude. The whole idea—by now quite large, with fourteen-foot-long crossed iron beams (the Morley-Miller instrument of 1905, essentially, with improvements)—the whole ungainly, clanky, awkward, yet somehow exquisitely sensitive arrangement gets hauled up into this purified situation. Such an unprotected, clear, and strangely pastoral situation as if seeking some kind of philosophical clarity as well. Should they have simply set it down out there in the pasture by mistake, gone off and left it, I doubt anyone, merely passing by, would have thought very much about it. It belongs out there like that—at least from a distance. It's a feeder, see, for cattle—buckets to dangle from the arms, or one of those pony-training things where they learn to trot around in circles. Or a carousel for kids. Who knows. You see all kinds of strange, abandoned mechanisms rusting away in fields. You think they must be agricultural, but it's hard to know for sure. There could be anything out there. The agricultural condition—the profundity, the clarity and simplicity that recommends itself to children's drawings and underlies the common experience of the world and its mechanics—must engender a kind of instinct toward invention. Miller himself enjoyed a boyhood on the farm. That little gate up there on the mountain probably squeaked the way such gates have always squeaked to the performance of one's chores.

When I was eighteen, my friend Steve and I decided to take a hike along the railroad tracks to the north as far as we could go. I think at that time, in the summer of '65, the tracks—a corridor of the Cotton Belt Route—were quiet, decommissioned, and about to be transformed into the weirdly warm-pink-sodium-lit Dallas North Tollway, which would draw our civilization north until there'd be no north of town anymore, no relaxation into distances, no clear and deep transition back to flatness from which cities and all knowledge must derive and into which, sometimes on weekend nights, we liked to take our girlfriends to go camping, as we called it. Come, we'd say, out into the fundamental lowlands of the heart, out Preston Road to the north then left down FM 544 and right on unmarked roads, some unmarked road, that ran out into all that cropland past those shotgun-blasted POSTED signs and the faint, suspicious glow of farmhouse windows, get as far out into all that as we dared, then pull off somewhere into trees or onto a rocky rise where we could have a fire and a bottle of wine and sit around and say whatever we could say and if love missed, as it generally did, it would keep going; you could sense it gently moving straight on out above the fields, the lines of barbed wire, angling above the dark low silhouettes of trees that lined the creeks and, totally massless, therefore heedless of the curvature of the earth, on out forever on a pure straight horizontal into the empty starry night. So, with all this in mind, I'm sure, and how it all would have to go—those girls would move and Steve would join the Marines and I'd be off to college—we decided we should take the clear straight cut along the tracks out north to get a clear straight sense of things as time was running out. My dad said sure. He rode the rails when he was young. Steve didn't need permission. He was pretty much on his own already—high-school-dropout motorcyclist. Very Fonze-like but for his stature, six foot two or three. I'm only five foot eight. So, in my mind there is a comically vignetted (like the end of a Charlie Chaplin movie) shot of us from behind, like Mutt and Jeff or perhaps George Washington and whatever comic sidekick he took with him to survey the vast frontier, as we departed pretty late in the afternoon from Lovers Lane to take the measure of the prairie to the north, my surplus backpack

stuffed with curious equipment—pyrotechnical flares, a foot-
and-a-half-long bayonet. Why in the world should I be telling
this? I think to get to the sense we had of venturing into an indistinct but somehow pristine state of things. Not tidy,
certainly—tracks through cities cut through all that sad, subconscious backyard clutter—nor do we ever actually make it
out to clear, continuous cropland. But a sense of being drawn
into a freshly opened seam quite close to home. The unused
tracks a sort of wedge into our day-to-day experience—our assembled understanding come apart along that line to spread
out flat like one of those cartographic projections where the
greater truth requires a certain distortion. I remember how, at
dusk, the hum of power lines took over. How the traffic noise
receded and this deep, uncomfortable murmur from the wires
between the huge high-tension towers that accompanied the
tracks set up what seemed a kind of privileged apprehension.
Not the sound of power usefully expended. But a strain. A vast
and unrequited hum into whose influence we had drifted. With
whose sentiment—How else to say?—we felt ourselves drawn
into parallel, and so grew silent for a while. A couple of miles,
maybe. Until the dormant rails and the power lines diverged
or terminated and we crossed a complex gathering of east-
west tracks and lines of idle railroad cars (to make way, in a
few years, for the Lyndon B. Johnson Freeway) to discover ourselves, at length, upon a dark and silent cultivated field of
blackland prairie, freshly plowed, than which there is no darker,
quieter natural surface. Nor, I think, one more uneasily tra-
versed. At least at night. Like empty space but corrugated so
you're always falling in and out of phase. You can't see squat.
As if whatever residual light should be left hanging in the air
gets sucked away. And sound as well. With the clear exception
of the sound a cowbell makes—which we were able, bedded

down among the furrows, to confirm at regular intervals all night long from various points about the compass, all within what seemed a fairly constant radius and without the slightest shift in tone or frequency to lend some qualification to the dark, to what my sleepless thoughts constructed as a pitiless tintinnabulating emptiness of furrowed prairie reaching out forever until morning. Had we not been quite so eager to depart, upon discovering we had camped almost beneath the eaves of the farmhouse, I believe we would have killed that cow for scientific reasons—there it stood not twenty feet away, a stupid child's drawing of a cow with a great big stupid copper bell. Is science everywhere? Like metaphor and tragedy? I think perhaps I'd drawn my bayonet, but Steve prevailed and off we went.

There's nothing much until about noon. Dirt roads or asphalt roads so crumbly I remember them as dirt. An outdoor faucet on the blind side of a tidy little house—and all the sweeter by itself out there like that. The house. The faucet. Now we're hobos. Now we're capable of stealing apple pies from farmhouse windows. Now we're ready, as the little unpaved road we've taken narrows to a double-rutted path, to hop the fence and head cross-country. Open country, it in fact appears to be. Whatever that means. A sort of feral ground, I guess. If one can tell by looking down. If one extrapolates from this discouraging patch of grassy, scrubby stuff right here on the other side of the barbed-wire fence on out forever to the north. So now it's noon. And here's that somehow pristine, disassembled state of things I spoke of—finally laid out flat, untidy, indistinct, and, after an hour or so, uncomfortable as the murmur of the power lines. Things come apart and you can feel an urgency. The way, with jazz, the melody becomes more clear, more precious, as it threatens to disintegrate. The whole idea of melody exposed and placed at risk. What is the whole idea of ground? An expression of the flatness at the bottom of the heart. That dark reflecting pool we're always gazing into. We're so tired. We're thinking maybe this was not a good idea. We are not thinking philosophically at this point. To the extent we think or speak at all it has to do with dung beetles. They are everywhere. At this stage (and I think by now we sense—not to articulate or anything—a vaguely Dantean structure to our journey), but at this particular level, they're the most conspicuous life-form. Holy crap, I think I probably actually said. Look at 'em go. I did not know what I know now, but I perceived I'd made a joke. Of course the crap part. Pretty funny. But the holy part as well. Here's what I know right now and what I may have had a faint awareness of back then. I've got my mom's old bright green copy of Sir Wallis Budge's transcript and translation of the *Papyrus of Ani* or *The Book of the Dead*, propped open on my desk to page 339. I'm quoting footnote number 2 and trying to imagine having had this book among the crazy contents of my backpack, having paused and set my backpack down to read while all around us we imagine we can hear this tiny, soft, and ancient skittering of the sun across the sky:

Kheperà was self-produced, and he was the creator of the world and of all on it. He was the father of the gods, and men and women sprang from the tears that fell from his eyes upon his members, and so became sources of life. His name in its simplest form seems to mean "he who existeth," "he who is," but in later times the verb derived from it means "to evolve," "to develop." The oldest symbol of Kheperà is the beetle, and the earliest conception of Kheperà was that he existed in the form of a gigantic beetle, which rolled the ball of the sun across the sky. The ball of the sun was regarded as the source of all life, and was compared to the ball of excrementitious matter which the *Scarabaeus sacer* collects, and rolls along to the place where its larva is so that it may feed upon it.

And imagine how I'd close the book and sit there on my backpack for a while. And we'd be gazing off and thinking what a penetrating, fearless intuition of the mundane path to heaven. You can't get any more mundane than "excrementitious." Do we hear it? Really? Maybe, if we sit here long enough. The sound the sun makes in translation. And another thing: a discovery published just this year in the journal *Current Biology* shows that dung beetles, who must roll their ball of dung away from the heap in as straight and rapid a course as possible to prevent its being stolen, are able to navigate by means of the Milky Way. No kidding. Think of that. They'd known for a while that certain kinds of beetles in the daytime use the sun or a pattern of polarized light that appears around the sun—and, given the ancient associations, how can it get any better than that? But, still, the Milky Way. The whole galactic plane. You cannot help but want to think of it quite closely and imagine it somehow—that it is possible to apprehend the instant of comparison or reception or whatever is going on. At night the dunghill black and deep as furrowed prairie. There's the quiet digging in, the separation. Nothing lower. Nothing less than this is possible. And then what? We must not pretend it's possible to know. And yet we do. The little eyes look up—or does he have to elevate himself, incline himself until a feeling enters in? Can we say that? Allow such notions to reduce to a sort of point? A certain feeling funnels down toward a solution—like a scribble, hearts and arrows on the ground. It makes you wonder, though, since these particular beetles are good fliers, if a glitch in the code or something might occasionally instruct a strange and marvelous reversal of the process.

Most of the day, then—until midafternoon—we cross this pure, undedicated emptiness we'd no idea was out here. Just an emptiness of the sort you'd find appearing in the alley, in the unmown space behind the garage, but spread out over miles, expanded, aggravated, getting in your shoes and burry bits all over your jeans. We shall escape before too long. We'll reach the edge and find a road that takes us out to 544 where an old brick church stands on a rise and a man on a riding mower rides round and round tossing plumes of yellow dust and giving us a little wave. And so dispiriting is this, somehow, that we toss it in and hitchhike back to Dallas. But before this, well before, as we are making our way across the terrible emptiness, we see this house, this leaning two-story farmhouse in the distance and behind it something shining—all spread out, complex, and shifting in the breeze. You can't have shining out here, can you? That's not right. But sure enough, as we approach what must have been a backyard once, distinct from the philosophical ground state that's reclaimed it, there are these things. These shiny, galvanized-sheet-metal, modern-arty constructions. Maybe four or five feet tall, most built to turn upon their bases in the wind. Some have these hoods like giant flared and crested gladiators' helmets. Others more like tents or kites—all open, seemingly presented to the air as if to take it in, to gather the expressions of the atmosphere unto the marvelous, vaguely scientific-looking shine of it. "Like shining from shook foil," in Hopkins's phrase, which I once thought so strangely, awkwardly descriptive of "God's grandeur," till I realized the brilliance of that reaching for and blasting through the lowest,

simplest, homeliest point of wonder. It would be years before I
learned that these things were cattle feeders. "Mineral feeders,"
actually, each to receive a plastic tub of bovine dietary supplement and be left out in the open, commonly fitted with some
sort of spinning, wind-directed shield to keep out rain. And of
course, although I don't remember any, there would have had
to be cattle out there somewhere. How, otherwise, the beetles?
But at this point we are tired. Worn out and captured in the
superficial moment. Drained of doubt. It is a bright, uncritical
wonder, this array out here like this behind the almost-certainly
empty, gaping farmhouse—blasted back to bare wood, leaning
toward that instant when the earth moves out from under, yet
not quite beyond the faint, strained possibility of life. I know
there was something—an article of clothing on a line, perhaps—
still bright enough to speak of human presence not quite finished, not quite given up all automatic movement. Something
like that made us think we'd best not hang around. That this
arrangement here was to be glimpsed and looked away from.
As, years later, I would come to decide was the way to regard
the strange, dark still-life paintings of Sánchez Cotán—so few,
all done around 1602, all black and cold beyond the cold stone
open window where the brightest things we love to see and eat
are placed or dangled on these strings as if to tease us or ad-
monish us for gaining such a glimpse of them, so brilliant
where they're kept in secret storage here, the best things in the
world, so brilliant as they seem just barely here, emergent from
the dark. It isn't anything, of course. It's just we're beat. It's just
the back side of the farming operation. Here, eternal, pure,
untidy, philosophical ground we like to use for forage. Here,
the house. And here, somewhere, the point where human life
departs. And here, the sky. And all this shiny, spinning, atmo-

spheric, instrumental business at the interface. For cattle, sure. For cattle.

By September 1924, the massive interferometer in its barn-like shed was ready, and the measurements began. It was a physical operation—very strenuous. And Miller was a small man. Again, I have to wonder how it felt. Though I must not pretend it's possible to know. Or that it carries any meaning— though it might. Can I say that? That much? There were, the following year, more data-gathering sessions (so exhausting, he himself would note) in April, August, and September, wrapping up at last in February 1926. He'd have to stand and actually shove this thing around—the mercury bearing helped, of course, but there was still inertial mass to overcome—through sixteen stations every circuit, every 22.5 degrees. A little bell would tell him when to stop and bring his eye up to the eyepiece for a measurement—an estimate of the amount by which the interference fringes' delicate vertical bands of bright and dark had shifted in relation to a pointer—which, called out to an assistant, would be entered. There's a pretty wide divergence of opinion, it would seem, as to the number of measurements taken. How many ringings of the bell (the hateful bell, you'd think, eventually). How many tiny, unfelt lurchings of the heart. I'm going to go with Fickinger's low-end calculation of about two hundred thousand. So, let's round it off to endless. How about endless. Gazing, one imagines, *at* (for a couple of thousand turns), then *through* the screen of lines. You can't maintain that sort of rigorous opacity forever. Pretty soon the world comes in—or at least approaches as someone standing on a screen porch feels the breeze and smells the rain before it gets here. There is that. What else? There's light through trees like riding on a train, say, through the country, late afternoon, and all the trees line up just right against the reddening light that flickers bright and dark across your half-closed eyes. Or getting lost out there in the corn or wheat. He must have done that as a child. But this, of course, so much more subtle. The interrogating means itself interrogated. Hoping for a slip. A flicker of something more than data, finally cold and pale as ash—all hope and data ground together fine as flour in this deeply horizontal sort of milling operation. And you note, of course, his name in this connection, how he works in this regard to turn this thing around and around the simplest question, over and over—milled to nothing almost (no one ever managed to reproduce his faint results or justify his faintly hopeful interpretation), ground to dust you can imagine settled out upon the ground as if to try to catch a footprint. "Are we here yet?" is, I think, what it reduces to. Can we be shown to have a proper motion through the dark, then we must have a place as well. I think that's it. And it's so close to simple knowledge, the requirements hardly any more complex than farm equipment—see, just turn this big old tractor axle sideways, weld those combine struts on there, then we can send off for the mirrors. If we even need the mirrors. If we even need to do this. What do you think? I think somebody already did this, maybe. Long ago, with light through trees or something. How light fades across the sidewalk in the evening, maybe. Something pretty simple.

———

GIVEN ALL THE CLEAR and rigorous direction of *Tom Corbett*—all that struggling verticality, that strict, wide stance and arms-akimbo military stuff; straight up, straight down—there was about the gentle, horizontal thrust of *Space Patrol* a more sustained and more specific act of will. You had to lean into it.

Something I have noticed about the way old people drive. How far ahead they seem to look; how close they press against the wheel. Do I do that? I may be getting there. I'd like to see what they see, in a way. I'd like to gain that sense Commander Corey has of unimaginable distance, light-years, zillions of light-years, crossed while leaning on the stick, the yoke. While peering ahead into it. Pressing on into the dark. As if such distances might be anticipated. "Are we here yet?" On and on. He grips the stick. He has to know what he is doing.

AN ENCHANTED TREE
NEAR FREDERICKSBURG

1.

THE FRIEND I TOLD THIS STORY TO INSISTED I WRITE IT DOWN.
He is kind. And thinks there may be kindness in it. But I'm not
so sure. I tend to get excited on the phone—he lets me go and
I get all jazzed up in telling this, and sure it actually happened,
it's all true, but still, you have to understand I'm in the oral
tradition here, and pacing back and forth and probably making
gestures he can probably infer. And bringing everything into it,
getting back to it myself. And here the actual truth of the matter is assumed to be subordinate. Oh, this goes way back, you
know. This letting the story be the thing. Can you imagine?
Back before the reflections on apples and eyes were shaped like
tiny windows. Back before the little arrow that we draw between the object and its utterance knew for sure which way to
point on all occasions. It's that back-and-forth, that sloshing
out, the spillage of the meaning that seems generous, I guess.
And possibly kind. I'm not so sure.

There used to be a single tree atop Enchanted Rock in Texas.
It's a pretty popular tourist spot. I'd been here once with my

kids and thought it quite remarkable—the huge granitic dome as if some asteroidal body were emerging. And it does, as one ascends, begin to feel like you've set foot upon an alternate possibility. A simplified expression of the world before our eyes acquired the windows we observe it through today. Above the rubble at the bottom, which supports all sorts of scrub and scattered oak, mesquite, and cactus, where the deer will come to browse at dusk, it all gets pretty strange. It all emerges as a simple, vast convexity of granite, bare and singular. A single thought at work, arising here above the muddle, the default, the general endless settling out we've come to think of as the ground, as fundamental. On the rock, though, it gets fundamental. Oh, my goodness. Huffing and puffing your way up, you sense that the greater struggle isn't so much against the slope as against the change of thought, the shift in reference. Whatever it is, it takes some climbing. So, on this particular visit, this ascent, my second I think, and long enough ago that the tree atop the rock had yet to fade and curl away into a stump, my friend the artist Doug MacWithey, his friend Karan (later, gradually, his wife), and I had paused about halfway up. He needed to rest. We wouldn't know for years how bad it was with him, his heart and everything, the horror of his childhood having beaten him up so badly he insisted that his wit (a truly transcendental goofiness—he'd sing Sinatra's "My Way" in the voice of Donald Duck with such ridiculous sincerity it almost made you cry), but that his wit, his grace with silly crowds at openings, was essentially apotropaic, a word I taught him, and compensatory. Anyway, he felt the need to rest. While I, on my part, felt the need to be a jerk and so agreed to meet them later, setting bravely, ostentatiously off for the top.

The spoken version, how you tell it over the phone or in the mead hall, is more spooky and direct. The other climbers, other tourists with big hats and water bottles, are not mentioned. Nor, I think, that I had been up here before and noted the tree all by itself—that scrawny, twisty little oak—at the very top. Though merely noted; there were kids who needed watching. Nor, in fact (for at the time it was not clearly understood), that the phenomenon at issue, the essential apprehension of the story, is not technically, arboriculturally, even possible as interpreted. The oral version comes through Anglo-Saxon, blurts its way straight to the top to find the tree, among the shallow vernal pools, a spectral object right away. There is no doubt. No time to wander around up there with all the tourists holding their hats on in the wind. We're drawn directly to the point where love cuts in, whereby the vision is received and that is that. And that's enough to stun the rowdies in the mead hall into silence.

But, in fact, it took a while. I figured maybe I should go back down and check on Doug. But, as I say, we'd no idea at that time. How much rest he really needed. How loss builds up like cholesterol or barnacles or something. So I waited by the tree. And finally noticed, lightly touching, where a pocketknife had scraped the bark to make a place to carve a heart around two sets of initials. Still quite legible. And others too, less clear, about the trunk. And if you looked close you could see, along the two main branches, older ones—the heart shapes darkened, healed but still detectable; initials, faint intentions, nearly gone. How about that. Here is where they come. The granite, much too hard and coarse, would wreck your blade. A stuttery scratch is all you'd get. To scuff and wash away in no time. By the time you reach the bottom, get back home, get into bed, and send your thoughts up here, it's gone. No kindness there, I think, for sure. And spray paint seems so loud and gets you into trouble. Who would want to close his eyes, her eyes, at night and think of that? I had to strain a bit, to squint and look away and look again to see the higher branches, tertiary branches, nearly black against the sky. I'd shift my angle, lift my hands against the glare—I could have climbed up to the first split for a better look, I guess, had I not feared some sort of citizen's arrest. But it was clear enough—and here's the apprehension, here's the vision that defies all arboricultural understanding—that the scars, the little heart-shaped memories of love, were up there too, just barely, smaller, fainter, taken up the way the body moves old wounds along and why (so strangely, it once seemed to me) they give those beautiful gold-and-purple-enameled heart-shaped medals (Was I wounded? Yes, of course. I have this medal), like a valentine to come across and not remember anything about it but the loss. There was no other way to think of it. The hearts move up and up until released, somehow. Old lovers lie in bed down there and touch their hearts and feel the fading scars like vaccinations. Holy moly. I went skittering down to Doug. He looked all right. He made a joke. This is no joke. Get up. You want to know where love goes? Sure you do. We all do, right? I looked at Karan. Right? Of course. Of course. Well, this is it. Come on. So, up he got. And forth we went to see this marvel, to acquire this understanding of which, to this day (notwithstanding some research and consultation with Doug's brother Kevin, an arborist who actually lives down there in Fredericksburg, about the way trees grow, not like we do but from the very tips of branches), I will not be unconvinced. If Doug were here, he'd tell you too. He'd tell it straight. And all the sad old drunken warriors in the mead hall would fall silent.

2.

ATOP A VAST AND SMOOTH AND OTHERWISE BARREN ROCK AS BIG AS A mountain stood an oak upon whose surface had been carved by countless lovers countless hearts surrounding names or pairs of initials. Something about the grand reduction, the finality perhaps, of this arrangement seemed to have acted to constrain the amorous impulse to a regulated flow. A certain urgent uniformity of gesture—though not rigorous; exuberances in terms of scale or ornament were visible here and there, but overall it made an orderly release. It was as clear as it could be—from trunk to branch, love carried up into the sky, a rising plume like one of those oil-field towers flaring off the volatiles. The fresher, clearer, hopeful hearts below, with, higher and higher, older and older, tighter and darker scarifications, all but healed, erased, released into the elements, the constant wind, among the higher branches.

Now, it's true that trees are not supposed to grow like that—extend throughout their length—but rather only from the tips of recent growth. The trunk and branches grow not up but out—in girth. Love should not, therefore, hope for altitude but find itself fulfilled in its expansion, with the increase in circumference, toward a state of vague, benign illegibility. Specifics to dissolve, at last, within the broad intention, in the spreading heart-shaped smoke ring of the heart. Yet I am certain no one ever came away from that extraordinary place with any simpler, more intuitive understanding than the one I took with me—that love ascends and disappears. I can't conceive of any other. Unless lovers are imagined to have come equipped with ladders in those days, whatever days those were, and eager to begin at the very top. Which would explain the oldest declarations way up there like that. Which makes a very different story, I suppose. How love descends without disturbing any arboricultural principles. A top-down sort of thing. Like a siphon—you just get it going. Then it comes. Just keep it coming. Coursing down. But that's no good. You're not the source. It might cut off at any moment. You're dependent and detached. Besides, it's awkward and unnatural and would have you lying awake at night reluctant even to touch the hand that's next to yours for fear it will have stopped. Which isn't how it goes at all. Love goes away, but not like that. The first and clearest, least explicable understanding is the best. Against all technical reports. Love rising, fading, flaring off. How sad and beautiful, the volatiles igniting. One imagines certain frequencies of light beyond the ones we normally see, in which the tree might be observed to burn, in fact. A barely visible, alcoholic sort of flame. Which can't be good for trees as trees. It can't last long—the tree itself, I shouldn't think.

And so it proved to be the case. A few years after my encountering the mystery, thinking I might write about it, I endeavored to look it up online expecting to find a site devoted to it or maybe a cult. But there was nothing. The rock was there, of course, all over the place—a famous tourist shrine. But not a word about the tree. Although I noticed, way in the background of someone's vacation shot, a blur that might have been it. So I began to thumb through everyone's vacation photos. Everything's online. There's no forgetting. No unconscious, no subliminal anymore. As if our eyes had got stuck open. No one ever goes to sleep. And sure enough, I'd catch these glimpses, distant silhouettes beyond some random moment entered into the racial memory. Here we are and there we were, can you believe it? Sure, I see you. I see all of you. But now and then a closer, dated shot and a progressive thinning out and dying back until one, dated March 14, 2005, with this warmly dressed old couple standing next to it—an "old dead tree," it's captioned. Here they've managed, with some effort I imagine, to ascend to the very top of this strange, solid granite planetary emptiness. But do they wish to have themselves remembered in the emptiness? Of course not. Let's go over by this old dead tree, this leafless, brittle remnant, so it doesn't seem so empty. So it feels like there is hope. Or once was hope. The wind has stopped. Her denim overshirt, his jacket, hanging open. Look at them—so there-by-the-grace-of-God, so far from knowing, caring how they look, so simply standing and residual like the tree. We are residual, after all. It's how we are and what we do. "A young Chinese man took this photo . . ." After they took one of him. You see? The whole world knows to stand next to the tree, alive or dead, in these bleak circumstances.

3.

WITH REGARD TO THE ENCHANTED TREE REPORTED TO HAVE STOOD atop Enchanted Rock near Fredericksburg, and which has been described as bearing countless carved memorials, generally hearts enclosing pairs of names or initials, that, in apparent violation of the rule whereby trees grow, in linear terms, from the very ends of branches only, seemed to ascend with age from trunk to branch and so forth steadily upward, growing fainter till they disappeared, as it were, into the air in a sort of diagram of love's transcendent vanishing—regarding this, there is an explanation that preserves, perhaps, both science and appearances.

It is natural to suppose the earliest carvings would have appeared upon the trunk. And that the later ones (maintaining the established arboricultural understanding) would have had to find their place a little higher. Newer above and older below. Then, to explain how it might come to appear the opposite were the case—that love, all love, begins below and naturally carries, with the growing of the tree (in ways it's not allowed to grow), into the branches, up and up and older and older until released into the wind—we need to grant a pair of conditions. First, that the evidence—the coverage as a whole—is of some age. And second, that it represents, in its entirety, a limited event. Let's just assume that all this clambering up and carving of memorials occurred as a florescence, a sort of eruption of desire among the youth of scattered, lonely towns and ranches down below. A rush of feelings normally insular, discouraged and expended in that dusty central Texas isolation, suddenly loose for whatever reason, quietly gathered into a self-sustaining confluence toward expression in what must have seemed the most exalted way. If we allow that what we have here is the record of a passing moment—which seems to accord with observation that the freshest-looking markings were already fairly old—then we've a shot at making sense of this.

Trees grow, throughout their length, in girth of course. Each year, as we all know, another ring is added. So, the surfaces of trunk and branch expand, although at relative rates that vary with circumference. Thus the girth of a branch the size of your arm might double in a few years while that of the trunk would seem to have increased, as a percentage of diameter, only slightly. Any sentimental carvings, therefore, correspondingly more or less distorted. More or less healed, and therefore aged, with those below retaining clarity much longer than the upper ones, especially somewhat smaller, somewhat desperate, tragic, comic ones on secondary branches carved with acrobatic difficulty and perhaps less care and all the more exposed to the elements as well. Thus it might not take very long before you've got this false impression that love rises to its vanishing. Ascends like Roddy McCorley, in the ballad, to his hanging "proud and young." Is that all lost, then? Is transcendence thus disqualified? Do Roddy—golden ringlets 'bout the hemp-rope—and our love just go away? How can that be? We're left with this. Must we depart without inflection? What if we learned that Jimmy Durante, at the close of his fifties TV show, so famously receding, to the melody of "It's Time to Say Goodnight," into the dark along that spotlit path—the Great Schnozzola pausing in his trench coat, schnozz illumined, chiaroscuro, in each spot to bid farewell as if it were the end of everything, of comedy and tragedy, to turn and throw a kiss, to touch his slouch hat, tug his coat, and, finally, standing in the last little spot of light, to touch his hat again and turn into the dark—what if we learned that, for some technical reason, it had been filmed backward—kinescoped instead of live— and what we saw was a reversal of the truth? Would he have lied? Would Jimmy Durante, one of the greatest, saddest jazz pianist-comics in the world have lied to us?

CEREAL PRIZES

—

I SUSPECT A BROADER MEANING TO OUR BREAKFAST CEREAL back in the 1950s. To the ritual with that dreary, quickly soggy, deeply comforting stuff we loved as kids, depended on as antidote and sacrament against the differentiated terrors of the night. To that and all accreting to it—the marvelous offerings on the outside of the box and even, now and then, inside; just trinkets, sure, but so remarkable recovered from the sameness, from the spillage. There were powerful feelings that attached to this, somehow. As if all the comfort and the terror of the whole world were involved in having breakfast every morning. I remember this terrific sort of longing, but the meaning has escaped. I think such meanings shot right through us like neutrinos at that age. We were set up more as detectors than recorders. So extraordinarily sensitive to meaning yet transparent to it, I suspect profundities passed through us all the time. We knew all sorts of deep, important things but only very briefly. What I'd like to know is what might be required to get it back. What sort of action might be taken to reconstitute the moment, those conditions. Like, say, standing on a windy day in a field of wheat or corn and reading Homer. Something crazy.

What's the language for such meaning? What did Greek sound like back then?

The other night I'd barely started this and found myself jammed up. I had this title: "Cereal Prizes." It was late. Nancy was here. And I decide I have to have a limeade—one of those carbonated limeades with a chunk of lime tossed in to show it's real or almost real—from the Sonic drive-in down the street. Oh, nothing else will do for a jam-up at that hour. Want a limeade? She declines. So off I go—and on the radio, on NPR, a young man is speaking about his life. It's in the middle of the interview. So I don't know who he is or if he's famous. Why he's speaking. But I'm captured by the sort of graceful fright of it—how his language seems to have a kind of built-in resignation, seems to move toward some fatality, like opera. Medium limeade, please. Is that all? What else is there? Nothing. Nothing. Thanks. No problem, as they say. They always say. But there are terrors in the night. And this young man on NPR is talking about them. And he's speaking in this way, this casual way that seems to slide across events, that I imagine has to come from such a vigilant simplicity the language forms around the need to clear the view, to hold yourself away, not let the words catch on to things, not get caught up in specificities, unnecessary, unbecoming twists and knots that bind and slow you down and make no difference in the long run. Here the words must run together like a single thought, inflected where they need to be, like music but continuous like radar so if something really important shows, it shows like blazes. Gunshots, he's describing. How he lives with them. And how he'd rather not. How he would like to sit on his stoop all day if he wants and not get shot. A guy got shot. And he was there, this young man speaking, passing by. And there's this guy all shot up, lying in the street—and here's the part that can't be said, I think, in any other language in this way and have this meaning, this Homeric sort of sense—he says the holes, the bullet holes, that killed this guy are in himself. Not *as if* in himself but *in* him. They are *in him*. And perhaps he means the future but he also means right now and possibly always. I don't know. I'm in my driveway with my limeade. And I guess I chicken out and turn it off.

That night I'm wakeful. She's asleep, but I say, "Nancy?" She's so beautiful and kind, awake or asleep. She doesn't wake up easily, but if I say her name she finds another circuit somewhere and comes instantly and practically awake. And so I tell her about the young man on the radio and what he had to say about his life among the terrors and the dead guy in the street and how his language seemed the only possible language to address such things, as if it had developed over centuries to do so, and if sometimes it was difficult to understand, it's easy to imagine thus with Homer, how a listener might have lost the high and ancient Greek at moments in the song when passions lifted clear away from ordinary understanding. And how here I am discussing cereal prizes. Good night, Nancy. Holy shit.

The ones I'm talking about, the prizes, were the ones that came in the box. Not the ones you had to send away for—those were "premiums" and attached an altogether different set of feelings; not so deep, the surprise and mystery lost in the weeks it took for them to arrive. I mean the ones you'd find in the cereal box itself as if by accident, like finding them on the ground. On the street. That something-out-of-nothing sort of power and unlikeliness—to which a child, so recently produced out of that powerful unlikeliness, would be especially sensitive.

My friend John Lunsford, a former museum director and teacher to me in my youth, who retains, in spite of age and erudition, much of his childhood sensitivity, has given me his

"Episodes with Zuni Ancestor Spirits and Gods," an account of his recent expedition to the annual Shalako ceremony of New Mexico's Zuni Pueblo. It begins with a simple paragraph within whose plain description is a broader understanding:

> All of the main streets in Zuni Pueblo are paved, unlike at the time of my first visit in 1962. Even today, however, the secondary streets and passageways are all in the clayey Zuni soil, and thus remain rutted and uneven. At eighty, one has to watch one's step, and this year, on December 7, 2013, as is usual in December, residual, or larger, patches of ice add to the need for care in navigating the ways to shrines, or to certain of the houses chosen annually as one of the six Shalako houses.

As he comes across "the clayey Zuni soil" it all goes softly metaphorical to me. It's just a whisper but sufficient to suggest the larger risk (like the beginning of a Lovecraft tale—"When a traveller in north central Massachusetts takes the wrong fork . . .") that's involved in such a visit, such an ambivalent invitation, to observe a different vision of the world. John knows to watch his step, and how to keep his deferential distance in all circumstances—no less at the trading post or the visitors' center than along the margins of the ceremony, sometimes in its shadow. His meticulous and naturally generous gaze seems to enlist all in a kind of metaritual, a sense of the miraculous emergent from the commonplace. This is ancient stuff. It happens where it happens. And so strangely in the middle of the day, right in the middle of a dirt road where some rock that's always been there with the cars and dogs and daily operations passing over it now reveals itself to be the sacred focus. Here they come—the striped and speckled, masked and feathered

higher powers, with their rattles and their mystifying utter-
ances to sway and shake and turn about and place, beneath the
lifted stone, their offerings. And pretty soon they're gone, and
with them all the ritual-cornmeal-tossing Zuni who had gathered, leaving the rock back where it was and one to wonder
where the other sacred shrines might happen to be and in what
seemingly random, unaccountable ways the unaccountable in-
tersects to trip us up and to remind us that it's all right here, has
been here all along.

But what gets me even more than this in John's account is a
moment shortly after dark as he and his friends await the arrival of the Shalako themselves from across the river—which
goes dry at times and, John confirms, is usually much as shown
in the early photographs and paintings, hardly more than an
extended muddy puddle without proper banks or structure;
though John says, since those old photographs, they've built a
decent footbridge for the crossing of the gods, who have descended from the sacred mountain a couple of miles away, over
to our side of things. The Zuni side. They come across the
puddle like it's nothing. Like that rock. Why should that make
it so exhilarating? Something out of nothing. Like those wild
Homeric street gangs, drive-by shooters, that the young man
on the radio was telling us about—all at the dangerous verge of
myth. Of epic poetry. His language like a poetry invented to
exalt the random terror of it even as it seeks to find a distance,
an escape. Did Pasolini, in Medea, mean for Jason and the Argo-
nauts to come across as street toughs on a raft?

But, anyway, John and his friends are out there waiting at
the edge of the Zuni village in the dark, about to freeze but
listening, now, to birdlike calls and sounds of chanting. Now
the Shalako are coming—ten feet tall with clacking beaks and
rolling eyes as big as grapefruit. These are crazy-looking gods

with no concern for human sympathy or sympathetic affect. They come looming, swaying into the beams of headlights from the cars along the other side of the river. You'd think candlelight or torches but it's headlights like they're deer or something sudden, unexpected. Like an accident. The terrible reality you hate to have to see. What sorts of things get caught in the headlights? Nothing pleasant. Headlights shine on things you'd just as soon not deal with. Things that aren't supposed to be there in the road or on the bridge. John says it's stunning. Sometimes blinding with the beams directed toward you, casting you into the uninterpretable shadows of the gods.

I think, as children, we have the code for all of this, if not the formula, the language. And it doesn't take too much to set it off. As if significance—the abstract possibility of meaning (let's allow the faint redundancy of that if we allow it in ourselves—the you that's you and then the you that knows it's you)—as if significance, as a pure abstraction somehow, filled the air and only waited to condense. And as a child you've no instructions, no resistance. Here it comes. You plunge your sticky little hand into the cereal and here it is, whatever it is. Whatever arbitrary thing upon whose surface meaning glistens like the dew. The Cereal Prize. It sounds like something ancient—having to do with gods at the harvest, meanings bright and terrible. And maybe it was like that in a way.

A few remain quite powerful to me. The army patches in boxes of Rice Krispies or Post Toasties or whatever. There were ranks. You might get private, corporal—sergeant if you were lucky. Quite substantial and authentic-looking. Smaller than the real ones. But real stitching, real embroidered yellow stripes, as I recall, on canvas ground. You could iron them onto your jacket or your T-shirt. I knew a kid who got a staff sergeant patch and wore it all the time as if he'd actually earned the rank. And, in a way, it seemed he had. Three stripes, one rocker, I believe. We loved to contemplate the heady possibilities. All the way to first sergeant, I think. At least in principle. Imagine one of those ironed onto your T-shirt—too many stripes and rockers to count, with that little diamond in the center. Way too big for your sleeve; you'd probably have to iron it on the front and then, oh goodness, parents, teachers, Eagle Scouts will step aside. One is invested and complete. There is no longing anymore. There's only you and the U.S. Army and around it all a sort of timeless mist.

Then there were those little cards with images from *Space Patrol,* the Ralston (Rice Chex, Wheat Chex)–sponsored TV show. Baseball card–sized cards with "negative" pictures (white on black) of the principal characters, planets, rocket ships, and such. You were supposed to stare at the image for a while, then at a white wall or the sky, and there would appear a fleeting positive afterimage. I didn't care too much for Ralston products, though I loved the show, so I remember only the card from that one box. It was a rocket ship. No problem there. I went outside and stared at it while slowly counting to thirty as instructed, then looked up and there it was. As if descended through the clouds. As if I'd passed some sort of devotional meditation test or something. My novitiate or something. Something wonderful in any case. I think I must have made a habit of it, sought the vision in the sky with regularity, because I know, at some point, I no longer needed the card. It would just be there on its own. I'd gone too far and burned it in. For years, as styles of spaceships changed, it hovered, needle-nosed and scythe-finned, way up there like some religious cult delusion. Until sometime in my thirties, when it seemed to lose coherence as a spaceship and to join the other natural small afflictions—specks and "floaters"—I'd begun to notice entering my vision, and a tendency toward which might seem a better explanation from the start.

And then, of course, the one that turns it all around and takes it right back to the pre-Homeric landscape, back to the street, back into the clayey Zuni soil. It was the deed to a single square inch of land in Canada's Yukon Territory that came in boxes of Quaker Oats Puffed Wheat, although I don't remember much about Puffed Wheat. I must have bought it for the prize. And more than once, I should imagine, since the whole idea became a sort of land rush. Lucky the lad whose aunts and uncles liked that stuff, who could inherit without the sacrifice, the tedium, or the shame of surreptitiously exhausting the supply by other means. It was a little like those afterimage cards in that we found ourselves directed to look elsewhere for our actual gratification, though the elsewhere in this case—not only distant but deferred, and even a bit abstract; the Yukon stood for cold and distant, hardly more real than Timbuktu in our minds—placed even greater demands upon the imagination. We would gather, each of us separately, our certificates together (so peculiar, this required more territory than was promised), spread them out or line them up to find some sense of an accumulating fact—of place or something. Even coming to understand the vast unlikeliness that any two square inches were contiguous, might there not still be a way to shuffle these around to make a sort of place? The way a kid thinks of a place—which is to say, a place to be? Such efforts seemed to render each square inch more isolated. More a concentrating focus upon the cold and bleakness. What had happened here? We thought the whole point of the cereal prize was to be plucked, like an act of grace, from bleakness. From the sameness, from the comfort and the tedium. Not to clarify it or focus in upon it. "Here's your property, little man," the Quaker Oats man seemed to say, with a chubby half-smile like the Buddha's. (Quakers, Buddhists—weren't they pretty much the same?) "See what you think. It's all right here."

What would they think, your aunts and uncles, if they knew? You'd lie awake at night and thumb through your collection in the dark, each deed permitting you to imagine bringing one eye up from underground ("from underground" is how the Zuni say they entered the world) to see, from within your one square inch, the cold gray sky. And all the other kids, you figured, just like you, out there somewhere as cold in the ground as you, amazed monocular gazes beaming up like flashlights. Flip a card and look again: it's all the same square inch, the time, the place, the cold gray sky, the gaze. What kind of cereal prize is this? To turn us back to the emptiness? I think it's not recoverable. I think we probably knew, for just a moment, then forgot.

PAPER AIRPLANE FUNDAMENTALS

———

LIKE TO USE THE SAME PAPER I TYPE ON—LETTER-SIZED, thirty-two-pound. It's heavy enough to take all the erasing, bulks the stack so I feel I've done more than I have, and holds the crease where the wings fold out so there's not quite so much give and flutter in a gust. You don't want flutter in a gust. You lose your lift.

It's strange to me that most people don't make paper airplanes. Don't know how. Or if they're pressed by their kid, they'll come up with some goofy-looking, pointy thing with these sad, vestigial tabs, these curious afterthoughts, for wings. You don't want afterthoughts for wings. The kid goes off and tries to fly this thing. Like trying to throw a potato chip. There's nothing to be gained. There's only sorrow. It should be like Greek and Latin used to be: you need to know this if you want to be a proper, thinking person in the world. If you would sense the subtle, fluctuating buoyancy of history and knowledge. Gain the pleasure and the insight that derives from watching falling leaves for more than that hypnotic resignation that descends on us each fall—for that, for sure, but then within that to appreciate those unforeseen stabilities, departures from the tumble when a leaf of just the right configuration catches air and finds the wind and sails away. You want to know what that's about. You want to feel it. Kind of go with it yourself.

Among my friends from childhood, no one had a better feel for buoyancy and balance than Vernon Grissom. He played oboe in the junior high school band. He had this trick he'd pull while playing—notably once in one of those big-deal annual concerts with the auditorium packed so there was nothing anyone dared try to do about it. Slowly, as he played, he'd lean his chair back, lift his feet, and simply balance there like that. On two legs. Playing. For the whole performance, I believe. The other players wouldn't look at him. Or, I suspect, allow themselves to think about it. Had he actually floated there a little above the stage, I don't imagine he'd have generated any more anxiety or prayer. And then of course it was the oboe—high and delicate like the sound of air escaping from a small balloon. The tension was astonishing. The gestures of the conductor, band director Mr. Fox, acquired an unaccustomed fervor in his efforts to impart, it seemed, a certain accelerando. Whispers spread among the audience. And by the end—I wish I could remember what they played; there are such glorious possibilities—there had occurred a synthesis of earnest imprecision and this clear, sustained, perfected, and transcendent risk within it. To the extent that, as the band director slumped and Vernon touched back down, the audience rose as one in acclamation. Admonitions were subdued. I'm told that once, at the Texas state fair, on the ancient wood-framed Comet roller coaster, long since vanished, Vernon stepped from his car at the top of the first big rise and waited there—I can't imagine what there was to stand on—for the next little train of cars to come along and let him in. And this at night. The Comet had been there, at the southeast end of the Midway, since the forties. As you clanked to the top of the seventy-foot rise, to your left there was the crazy, noisy dazzle of the fair, and to your right just darkness mostly—just a parking lot and then the sad, faint lights of blighted neighborhoods continuing, it seemed, on out forever that direction. And the Comet in between. It was a terrifying structure. You could see how old it was. How oft repaired. And oft repainted—cracking layer on layer of white. Like milk or ghee, in certain Jain and Hindu rituals, poured over saints or snakes in veneration or placation—but in any case to preserve us all and keep the rickety framework from collapsing. Which, when standing near it, seemed a possibility. Right under it was grass and, strangely, sheep. I guess they were there to go where a lawn mower couldn't—in among the forest of supports. And yet it seemed so odd, to have those sheep down there as if to introduce a note of calm. As if to let you know no matter how afraid you were, how bad it got among the clatter and the screaming, there were sheep. I like to think that Vernon stood there facing out across the parking lot, away from all the noise, into the dark. Old photos show a sort of rail, so maybe that was there to lean against. A flimsy length of two-by-four to feel the shake of everything, his gaping friends and everything, receding. Screams like real screams. Dark like real dark. And the sheep down there, attending to their business. Oh my goodness, here was buoyancy and risk to beat the band.

Sometimes on Saturdays we'd meet downtown. I'd take the bus. His mom would drop him off. We'd start at the library, find a table on the mezzanine, and spread things out—whatever he had brought in his briefcase, usually. Books and articles pertaining to astronomy, aviation. Paper airplanes if he'd thought up new designs, as well as paper to make more. Lunch at the Copper Cow, then on to the Southland Life building—Dallas's tallest at the time at forty-two stories, with an observation deck from which we'd fling our paper airplanes one by one into such powerful, unpredictable currents swirling around up there most got flung back or sucked straight down the side of the building. It could take a number of tries to get one out into clear air, into an updraft or a thermal where your heart would sort of hang to see it dip and flutter, stabilize and curl into the upward circulation, rise and rise so high that, were you on the ground, you would have lost it, would have squinted at the sky awhile then turned to go back in to make another. Or just sit and think about it. Have a glass of milk and a Hostess CupCake maybe, in the kitchen by the screen door where the air comes through in summer with the sounds and smells it's always had, and will for your whole life, don't you imagine, just like this, the air like breathing in and out the same breath, always and forever.

———

AT SOME POINT WE ARRIVED at what we felt was the best all-round design. The "standard model," as I've come to refer to it—as if what we are dealing with is a theoretical matter, a hypothesis. And maybe it is in a way, as long as it's topologically pure—no cuts, no tape, no added parts—which is to say it should be fold-able back into a sheet of typing paper. Which is to say (in a math-ematical sense, I think) identical to it. Thus, not only emerging from but entirely consisting in that flatness it escapes. From which it ascends. A model of consciousness, perhaps, in this regard—or, if you like, the soul—so long as basic aerodynamic principles are observed. What we arrived at was a simple modi-fication of the traditional blunt-nosed type—as distinct from the even more traditional pointy delta that most readily comes to mind when people think of paper airplanes. Pointy deltas look like darts. They are for distance, not duration. They will generally go where thrown. They're not expected to escape, to sail away, except in a gale or maybe a television commercial. In the classic delta all the folds converge along the longitudinal center, all concerns directed forward. Air is passive, to be penetrated. Not to be engaged except as bare, essential lift. The pointy delta is not borne aloft. Aloft is just an ancillary consequence of purpose. When you throw it, you don't follow it. Not closely, sympathetically, reflectively. The pointy delta flies into a future that is imminent, direct, and nonrecursive. One moves on to other things.

The standard model, like its blunt-nosed predecessor, starts with a big diagonal fold across the centerline, then back the other way—it looks, at first, as if you're going to make a boat or a little hat. It's indirect. A sort of embryonic recapitulation of the airplane's evolution from these earlier, simpler forms. From boats and hats. Our modification, though, eliminates the asymmetrical structure of the wing (one side untidy with its double leading edge) by gathering both diagonal moves into a single double accordion fold that's hard to execute at first but gratifying. You think, Ah, here is a physical expression of a quality of air we didn't know about, as each hand undertakes its several, simultaneous duties to encourage inward curves converging gently toward the nose and toward controlled collapse and finally, slowly creasing into place. What have we captured here? A principle, an accident, of buoyancy implicit in the paper, in the flatness all this time? And self-confirming in the foldings now permitted—unavailable before—to concentrate more weight up front where you want it. You fold the wings (to get a wingspread somewhat greater than the length, unlike the delta), and that gathering of paper at the nose is like a knot—a kind of inertial knot to tie onto the air with no more purpose than just that—to find the empty air and hold it. It's recursive in that way. You tend to circle.

Vernon added a gentle airfoil—which the blunt nose (folded back upon itself) allows by freeing up the leading edges. He would take the front part of each wing and roll it over the edge of a table, back and forth until it took the curve, and then he'd smooth it out and let it relax a little. Curl the trailing corners up to act as elevators—just the slightest flip. And there you go. What happens now? Well, it depends on the conditions. Something's represented here—some greater accidental thing. About the time I managed to luck out of the draft and get myself back into college, Vernon left for California, where he found a job as an airframe mechanic and died in a motorcycle crash not long thereafter. You can see what's going on here, right? The unforeseen stabilities. The buoyancy. The darkness and the sheep.

THREE CARTOONS

———

What is that weird high desert Krazy Kat inhabits? Monument Valley, of course, in a sense. That's what we understand inspires it, or permits it. But that's not exactly it. It has to do, I think, with the idea of the empty page laid flat. The simplest possible description of illusory space, illusory ground upon which and above which the primordial facts—your geological marvels, heavenly bodies, trees and rocks and bricks and fundamental passions—all present themselves in marvelous instability, moving about and shifting shape one frame to the next. It's like the world before the moment of creation settled down. With everything a mere enclosure for its animating spirit. Everything a sort of joke, a sort of costume with a sort of god inside.

When archaeologists in 1904 discovered, in the ruins of a temple at Palaikastro on the eastern coast of Crete, a fragmentary hymn to Zeus inscribed on a broken slab of stone, it gave a glimpse into an earlier understanding of the god, and gods in general, than had any ritual text before. It took a while to get the implications, drag the meaning out from under the weight of well-established notions. Jane Harrison's *Themis,* her famous study of religion, starts with it—shows how, though the stone itself is not so old, third century maybe, the inscription revives something much more ancient even than the already ancient text: beneath the mountain, or as if beneath the mountain, where the oldest stories place his birth, a pre-Olympian god not importuned but summoned, brought into the dance to leap— that word is used again and again—to leap, to overcome the weight of earth and death and animate the vital possibilities. What must the world have seemed like then—unsettled. In all aspects clearly, vastly, starkly animate.

Krazy Kat, full page, December 18, 1918

HERE SITS IGNATZ MOUSE UPON A LOG, HIS HEAD IN HAND IN THOUGHT- ful, vocal confirmation of his disbelief in Santa Claus, as Krazy, from behind a nearby tree, observes and listens. "Oh-ho," Krazy says, "so 'Ignatz Mice' you is a li'l infiddle, heh?" Then off he scampers catlike on all fours—a capability he will lose as the years go by but here he's captured in mid-bound, clear space between him and his exclamation mark–shaped shadow, dashing over the hill so fast, so urgently he overshoots a bit into the following unruled moment, streaks between the discontinuous frames of reference straight into a costume shop (Have we seen this before?) that's built like a keep, a mausoleum. Stone-walled. Dark. What sort of costumes, what sort of whimsy do they hold in storage here? Then out he steps, as slow and ponderous in his Santa suit, as mythic and inevitable as before he was mercurial—nothing more than chance and impulse. "Gollix," he exclaims, "you got no ida how this outfit makes me feel Yule-tidish. . . ." And there is a massive authenticity about him that suggests, perhaps, a deeper iconography: the heavy lace-up boots, the stiff white bell-shaped Sufic

cap. An unaccommodating Santa like the golem treading forth
out of the ages. Meanwhile Ignatz ponders, "Yezza, it's the
bunk . . . I'd just as soon believe the moon is made of cheese."

It's noon. That cartoon default noon that seems to carry
equal clarity and risk. One thinks of the heated noontime visions of the early Desert Fathers so monastically exposed like
Ignatz out there in the flatlands on his log. The doubt that sum-
mons what it fears. Perverted longing. Why would he say these
things out loud and then just sit there? Do you think he knows
what's coming? We can imagine, between the frames, the way
it happens. Ignatz silent, turned to squint way down the road at
something coming in the distance, just a fluctuating smudge at
first like that famous scene in *Lawrence of Arabia*, the terrible,
slow mirage of Omar Sharif, like death, approaching on his
camel across the sand. It's Santa coming down the road. Can he
believe it? In broad daylight? Does the realization gradually coil
about him till at last released to spring his eyes wide open, as
we see, and shoot him straight up into the air at the epiphany,
its finger lifted: "Ignatz Mice!! Behold!!! I am Senta Klaws."
Whereupon poor Ignatz falls to the ground, repentant, face in
the dust before the apparition, which forgives him, bids him
rise and turns to go. And that would be that—Ignatz admon-
ished and enlightened, Santa returned to that dark costume
shop—were it not for Krazy's tail zigzagging out from under
his coat and trailing behind. A brick's to hand and Ignatz flings
it. "Pow." And Santa bursts into constituent particles—boots
and beard and cap—the whole constructed Santa flies apart as
Krazy, simple once again, protonic, floating at the center of
disintegrated myth, receives the gesture in the usual positive
way. The final scene repeats the first. "I don't believe in Santa
Claus, I'm too broad-minded, and advanced for such non-
sense," Ignatz for the second time declares. Yet from his brow a

single drop of consternation falls. The scenery has shifted, lighting changed. The mood is not what it was. The tree behind him now looks blasted, branches curling like burnt matchsticks. From the east (whence Santa came—let's call it east) the sky is darkening. Dark and ragged clouds move in. A storm is coming. What has he done? What's happened here?

Koko's Earth Control, animated, 1928

ON A GLOBAL WALKING TOUR, WHILE PASSING THROUGH DESERTED RE-gions, Koko the Clown and his dog come upon the control room of the world. It's simply there at the ends of the earth, a neoclassical funhouse. Standing open. It's amazing. Koko's hat flies off. The little dog's ears shoot up. They walk right in. The dog goes wandering off as Koko stops to contemplate an array of rotary switches by a window. There's an irising-in on Koko's hand about to pull a lever labeled "RAIN" and then he's looking out the window (which is blank until phenomena are summoned) at the shower. He's delighted and he turns to us and gestures with his thumb at what he's done. Now it's the lever labeled "DAY AND NIGHT" and the spangled dark descends beyond the window like a shade; night comes down and goes back up. But even stranger is this ordinary window in this place—and look how carefully it's drawn, unlike the zany and perfunctory controls, to be an ordinary window. Simple double-sashed and properly framed and silled, the raisable lower sash with a thumb latch where it should be there on top. This is the window that we look out every day. And maybe that's why it's left blank. What can it mean? Well, while all this is going on the little dog, whose name is Fitz I think, has found the master lever. It emerges huge and phallic from the wall like the erection on a herm. And why not? Kept like that, upthrusting, it maintains the vital principle. But throw it, pull it down . . . don't even think about it. Read the sign. And here's the really crazy part: Fitz does. He reads the sign. And not only reads it, fastens on it with another of those irislike vignettes where all you see is what he sees, and that's the sign. And as if that were not enough he climbs his own little dotted line of sight to get a closer look: "DANGER BEWARE. DO NOT TOUCH EARTH CONTROL. IF THIS HANDLE IS PULLED THE WORLD WILL COME TO AN END." How to explain what happens next? He's going to pull it. And it's not some mindless reflex. He is straining for the handle on the lever, just a little out of reach, that ends the world. As if at long last here it is—what he's been waiting for. There's no internal conflict. There's no pause to let the diabolical impulse rise within him, overcome his better nature. This is it—the very thing he most completely wants to do. When Koko shows up Fitz is dangling from the handle, and there ensues a terrible struggle. Even Koko—small of head and vast of feet—knows better than that. He comprehends, at once, the consequences. Reels before the prospect. Snatches Fitz from the handle, flings him down, admonishes, then gives him a paddling with a suddenly huge and phallic admonishing finger (I'll show *you* the end of the world. Right here's the end of the world) and finally tries to restrain him but it's no use. It's beyond all that. What part do you think Fitz fails to understand? Is it the part about the world or about the end? Are those two things, in him, so far apart, those two ideas, they cannot be syntactically related? What do you think has been communicated then? We see his actions are as purposeful, as happy, wide-eyed, frantic as had the sign above the lever promised pork chops. Can it be that everything he's ever wanted is confused somehow with its annihilation? Is it because, as anthropomorphic as he is, he's just a dog? He's just an animal? And at last it's inescapable. Fitz slips from Koko's grasp and sort of vanishes under his shadow. Under that permanent pool of black at Koko's feet. How perfect is that? He disappears beneath the shadow of the clown to emerge behind him, shove him away, and pull the lever. There's a little puff of steam or smoke, a valve released. An ancient piston moving. Fitz just stands there, paws to his face. He's done it now. And there's no format to what happens. There's no theme, no clear idea about the end. One's fears come tumbling out like multiple mistranslations of apocalyptic texts. The air is rent with lightning flashes, positive-negative, white then black, the whole world flickering like that, night and day confused. The heavenly bodies, loosed from their circuits, all go crazy and mean-spirited in a self-destructive frenzy. We see Koko on his knees in prayer, eyes heavenward, in the middle of a vast plain ringed with lunar-looking mountains. It is night but the light is shining on him. Where in the world is this? It is the circus at the end of the world, I guess. Back where he started in the spotlight in the center ring but oh how bleak, how ruined it is now. What gags are left? A couple maybe but not good ones—strange ones, ones to make the children want to leave. He scoops a hole and plunges his head in the ground like an ostrich but it's just as bad down there. Up pop two heads—his own (from a new hole, stretch-necked, terrified) and another one, a monstrous one with horns and fangs. The infernal regions—what a terrible thought—just under the surface. But the big joke's still to come. An incredible mix-up. Koko loses his head in the sand and, in attempting to retrieve it, grabs the wrong one. Look at him now. He is a monster. For a second he just stands there with the wrong head, with the monster's head, his white-gloved fingers spread like claws and question marks arranged in the air around him. Who is this, then? Kali? Gorgon? The Devil himself? It's the sort of formulaic pose you see on ancient coins—a running gorgon turns at the waist to face us just like this on a silver coin of Etruria. Very much the same schematic horror. Just for a second he's this monster. We couldn't stand it any longer. Then he tosses away the horrible head, regains his own, and wanders out of the scene.

More lightning flashes. Cosmic circuits shorting out. Now Fitz in inexplicable combat with a tree as the earth cracks open. Koko passing among some ruins. What are these ruins— realistic, sad, historical-looking ruins so absurdly in the shadow of a silly, cigar-puffing, anthropomorphic volcano? It's all crazy. It's completely nuts that the world should end like this, with no consistency at all. It all breaks down. The way we see it all breaks down. More cosmic flickering as bewildered, terrified, disembodied heads of Fitz and Koko loom and vanish. Now as if from space we see them jumping up and down at the top of the writhing, detonating world somewhere near Greenland. Then it goes. It just blows up. That's it, we think. But no, that's only one world down. There's more to come. See—he's just tumbled into regular, giant three-dimensional space. Plop, onto an ordinary windowsill. Whose windowsill we wonder, several stories over Broadway or whatever street that is down there with actual, panicked, three-dimensional people racing around and trying to hang on as the earth (the camera) tilts this way and that. Now he's inside, the window closed. We see him pressed against the glass. Outside the skyscrapers are falling. It's that window, isn't it. Same as the one before—proportions, framing, sill, and even the little thumb latch. Here we are back in the studio of course, where all this started. Don't you suspect, when drawing Koko in the control room, the cartoonist thought, Hey, wait a minute—how's he going to see the effects outside without a window? So he looked around and simply copied that one. Stuck it in. We look out that one, one last time.

A steady view across the city—no more herky-jerky camera—
toward the river maybe. Smaller buildings. Curl of smoke from
a factory in the distance. What an odd, reflective moment—
only a couple of seconds really, just this long sad shot of the
city, sad and dingy and resigned enough to make you think the
end of the world might not need special effects, might be like
this—a long slow evening, red sun setting over the Lower East
Side. Look at this now for a second, which is all you've got unless you push the Pause button, as I've done. It's as if they'd
paused, themselves, the makers of this film, and caught a real
glimpse of the end. Have you ever read Henry Roth's *Call It
Sleep*? I've read about it and I pick it up every couple of years or
so and think I really ought to read it but I don't think I could
stand it. Just the last page and the title and the cover—which
this moment where I've paused reminds me of—is enough.
The thought of that, like that of Koko as a monster, is enough.
The red sun going down on the Lower East Side and all that
guilt. The idea of that is enough.

And then they do a funny thing. They gradually superim-
pose the ocean over the city. What is intended, I suppose, is in-
undation. What you get, though, is equivalence. One scene
merges into the other. Horizontals correspond—the rows of
buildings, lines of breakers. It's the city or the ocean. As the
ocean. It's the same. And it's so gentle, which I guess is what's
so sad. But enough of that. We're not allowed to pause and sigh
for very long. The studio's shaking. Fitz and Koko—ah, there's
Fitz—are running around on the drawing table as it tosses back
and forth. They're trying to keep from falling off. Is this it, finally? Where's the inkwell? They should jump back into the
inkwell. That would stop it. That would make it all a dream.
That's how it works. So, is the inkwell like the ocean? Where's
the inkwell? There's no inkwell. There's no sunset. There's no

sad, sweet consummation. It's all crazy. It goes on. Now Fitz and Koko turn into ink—a little puddle on the blotter sloshing back and forth and soon to be absorbed into the ever-expanding consequences. End without end, we're finally left to imagine, to consider from the window that we look out every day.

Uncle Scrooge Comics #6, 1954

THE MOST PERVERSE AND PHILOSOPHICALLY AMBITIOUS OF THE UNCLE Scrooge adventures sets the mechanisms of greed upon what seems to represent a spiritual quest. It's got the customary image on the cover—Uncle Scrooge in his devotion to his money (taken together, all the covers from the fifties, there's a quality of allegory; I can imagine a series of Holbein wood engravings of Uncle Scrooge in his miserly observances, repetitious and inevitable as the famous *Dance of Death*)—but anyway, here's Scrooge with a wooden tub and a washboard actually laundering his money. Behind him, bills hung up to dry.

On the inside cover is the usual six- or seven-frame vignette, which further demonstrates Uncle Scrooge's profound skin-flintiness in a form intermediate between the emblematic and the extended narrative to follow. The joke in this case—and it's always a simple joke—is Scrooge's impatient determination to wait for the library and its free reading room to open rather than shell out five cents for a newspaper proclaiming his own big oil strike.

Now, on the facing page the real adventure starts, as many do, with Scrooge in his money bin among the piles of money, hills and valleys, shifting dunes and wadis of money, gently undulating, semiarid vistas—coins primarily, with sheaves of bills here and there like weeds or clumps of drought-resistant grasses poking through at the hint of spring. Who knows what's in the mind that finds fulfillment here? It's hard to tell what's going on. Of course we've seen how he disports himself, loves rolling in it, diving among the piles. And yet there's evidence of husbandry, a strenuous sort of protocol involved. A bucket of coins in the foreground with a dollar sign on its side. A money bucket. Left there for some reason on a little knoll of money like a bucket of sand on a sandy beach. In the distance, visible just beyond a low moraine, a wheelbarrow loaded down with a single massive, sagging money bag. And sometimes there is even heavy equipment, as in #11, for example (on whose cover Scrooge is ironing wrinkled bills): a bulldozer, idle in the talus of a distant mound with Donald Duck, who's visiting with his nephews, perched aboard, hands on the controls as if imagining how it feels to live and toil in a world of money—in his silly sailor suit, if he would have the heavy touch, the raw delight to do what needs to be done, to manage it, to not be overwhelmed, to hold, no matter what, the thought as crude and clear as thoughts of ancient ducks perhaps, of mythic ducks back when the real world must have seemed as bright and graspable as this, when ducks were ducks and maybe—who knows?—just emerging into wide-eyed anthropomorphism.

Right off the bat, though, something's wrong. Scrooge dashes, trailing anxiety droplets, from the money bin. He's flung aside his shovel. Have we nearly caught a glimpse of operations? What in the world could he have been doing? What improvements involving labor of that kind suggest themselves? And so compelling that he seeks refuge in them, apparently, from the practical requirements, all the business, all the daily, wild, exaggerated urgencies commensurate with his fortune and toward which he's being summoned by his harried, desperate, semihuman underlings.

A word about the underlings. The seldom-seen accounting

staff and file clerks. Like those more or less realistically rendered creatures—squirrels and birds and bugs and such—maintained in the unevolved state to provide a natural background, they belong to a sort of peripheral population. Not so much default, I'm beginning to think, as reserve. They're generally pink and pretty much human but for round, black animal noses and, occasionally, floppy ears. But just that much is enough to keep that world closed in, prevent it from opening onto ours the way the world of Warner Brothers comics does—I've got a 1953 *Bugs Bunny* here and, sure enough, it's just a cartoon-human-populated world with cartoon animal characters in it. We're the background population for the most part, fully, uniformly schematized—no rudimentary animal characteristics— and invited to imagine Bugs just popping out of his hole into our midst without apology or excuse because he can, because as soon as we allow that cartoon gesture (like a rumor, like a dream) all bets are off. So what's with Duckburg? All those people not quite people? We're invited to imagine, it would seem (and this is what my wife once told me made her anxious, even queasy, as a child when given Uncle Scrooge or Donald Duck to read), that we are implicated, drawn into it under certain conditions, forced to compromise, to take odd jobs, ignore the slight disfigurement.

But anyway, let's see. It looks like Uncle Scrooge has more than he can handle—third-world despots wanting bribes, absurd demands from every quarter, wheedling letters piled as high as piles of money. It's no better on the street. They spot him: fat lady bearing down with child in tow (it flaps behind her like a rag doll, little round nose still pink) for whom she seeks career advice; immense top-hatted, swallowtail-coated, spatted rich man blocking the sidewalk to remind Scrooge of a speaking obligation as, between his legs, Scrooge scampers to be grabbed about the neck by a screaming, bearded, rat-faced anarchist wanting a billion toward the abolition of wealth. This last requires an extra frame to set up the joke—and look what's happened. Look at the anarchist, bearing in mind that it's only 1954. He's drawn from the intellectual school—a shirt and tie beneath his sweater. And his rat face, though still pink, shows marked development, with its giant ears and pointy snout and chisel-like incisors, from the range of nonspecific background types. He's on his way to a full-blown character. "Rat-faced Anarchist"—one can only imagine how that might have played in the early fifties. It's as if the not-quite-people and the more-or-less-realistic-background-animals felt an impulse toward each other, needing only a little dramatic provocation to combine.

But this is crazy. Scrooge can't stand it. Back at work he flings the phone across the room. He kicks his money. He goes nuts. He heads for the park and takes up residence in a hollow tree. He wants to revert, wants to live the simple life of a squirrel, whose hoarding instinct he already shares, of course. No good can come of this.

At last his nephew, Donald Duck, shows up to take him to the doctor but before he can he has to coax Scrooge down out of the tree, which makes for a curious scene at one point. Donald stands on the other side of the low brick wall that surrounds the park and rests his arms on top as he reasons with his uncle. Scrooge has emerged from the tree and begun to descend. He's lost his top hat but still wears his spats and purple Dickensian frock coat or whatever you call that thing he always wears. He speaks, responds. His eyes are clear, not goofy spirals. He looks fine. Except he comes down like a squirrel—headfirst, his hands and feet spread wide to grab the trunk the way a squirrel would do. What seems so odd about it—even spooky in a way—is that his reason has returned. So his behavior isn't crazy, merely thoughtless. He forgets himself. Or forgets to regain himself quite all the way for just a second, just a frame—he's fully recovered in the next, perched on the wall, upright and ranting to his nephew. It's disturbing, I think in this case, to discover ourselves disturbed. That such a silly, oddly conflated figure as Scrooge (a sailor suit at least makes a kind of thematic sense) should seem enough himself to lose himself significantly. What sort of mordant stabilizes Uncle Scrooge? That we should catch our breath a little at his shift and sense this momentary transformation anything at all like Dracula's, say—that passage early in the book when Jonathan Harker, gazing out upon the moonlight from his prospect high in the castle, sees the Count emerge from a window just below and slither headfirst down the wall. Or, looking even further back to Pleistoanax, young king of Sparta during the Periclean Age, who, according to A. R. Burn, impeached for the venality of his commanders and "fined a sum which he could not pay," fled like a beast to haunted Arcadia to live for nineteen years in a house built half inside and half outside "the grim sanctuary of Apollo the Wolf-God"— imagine a sort of park—"where it was said that human flesh was mixed with the sacrifices, that he who ate it became a wolf, and that no beast cast a shadow."

Well, on the next page we find Uncle Scrooge in the hospital much subdued, with Donald, Huey, Dewey, and Louie in attendance as the doctor, bag in hand, preparing to leave, recalls having heard of a legendary valley hidden somewhere high in the Himalaya Mountains and inhabited by a people with no concept of wealth. That does it for Scrooge. His pince-nez flies off his nose. He leaps from his bed. It's off to India. Off on the same old mad, obsessive expedition. There's no difference in the style—the continent-hopping, mountain-climbing, *Junior*

Woodchucks' Guide–consulting race to secure the heart's desire
wherever it is. And it's where it almost always is, at the ends of
the earth in regions so exotic and remote the cartoon gesture
itself is strained, a documentary sort of accuracy seems to leak
in so you get these photographic panoramas: here are the five
of them emerged upon the Himalayan foothills, gazing up. You
wonder how Uncle Scrooge can maintain his focus in all this
and his desire not simply vanish, steam away in the thin, cold
air of actual mountains, stupas, great-mustachioed Sikhs with
human noses. Yet, if anything, they seem to gain in clarity, the
cartoon ducks, against this marvelous *National Geographic* sort
of background. It's the outline of the world that looks uncertain all of a sudden—uncartoonlike, sketchy, deferent to reality.
Standing there on the steps of a temple, all in a row, they're
clear as bells, as clear and strange as zoomorphic Hindu deities.
They can do whatever they want. They can't be stopped. God,
how I loved this part as a child. It hardly matters what they're
after. They're not likely to get to keep it. Hopes and fears will
cancel out and they'll return to life between the quarterly
issues—Donald Duck to a house like ours and Scrooge to his
money bin, the sweet ennui, the old dissatisfaction.

But for now they're really after it. They hire a plane to find
the valley, which is hidden below the clouds. No place to
land. They have to parachute. It's at this point (thirty years before the lives of Bushmen are identically disrupted in the film
The Gods Must Be Crazy—maybe somewhere there's a common
source, some folktale) that there occurs the thing that seeds the
tragic irony to follow. Uncle Scrooge, to summon his courage
(not to jump but to pay the pilot), pops a bottle of his nerve
tonic. Out the little open window flies the bottle cap. A separate frame observes its fall—receding plane above, the shrouded
mountain peaks below. Then off they go. The plane swoops

down beneath the clouds, ejects supplies, and then the ducks into what really ought to be an allegorical summing up, the last adventure, Scrooge having overreached this time, beyond desiring particular treasure, seeking finally to address the central problem, to idealize possession—here, as far from his actual money and its distractions as he can get, here at the antipodes of desire, he might at last assume a perfect form of ownership, become, as it were, completely self-possessed. And so he seems to bring himself to the verge of wisdom. Only a philosophical step or two away. "Here I shall be able to rest!" he proclaims, arms wide as he dangles from his parachute, "Here among people that have no desire for my wealth!" It goes no further. There's no mystical leap. His money bin, the untranscendent fact, like Dracula's box of native soil, is all that's really in his thoughts and, in effect, as we shall see, he's brought it with him.

Down they float into the funnel of the world. For a page and a half, ten frames, descending panoramically into what must be an immense volcanic remnant—glorious, vast Gustave Doré–like walls and buttresses of rock from among whose snowy ledges countless arcing waterfalls tumble and mist into the valley far below. They're only ducks but they might be angels. It's that serious. Look what's happening. You can see it before they do, though you need a loupe. You see that little swirl of something in the middle of the lake that's in the middle of the green and terraced valley in the middle of all this. That's where they're going. That's the focus. By the bottom of the next page it's apparent they're descending into a whirlpool. Well, that's it, you think. It had to happen. There goes Uncle Scrooge with Donald and Huey and Dewey and Louie along for the ride. No more new issues to go with your bowl of Thompson Seedless grapes and your orange juice when you're playing sick at home. You're left with the allegorical necessity, the lesson that desire extends not to but past your longings and that happiness, boys and girls, is an inattentive, accidental sort of thing like a clog in the drain.

I suppose we *could* have lived with that. But wait. A safety net. They're jerked right out of the center of this Dantean schematic, this admonitory vision (which is how we're left to think of it)—"Sprong!"—hauled in like fish and welcomed among the happy, duck-billed, but otherwise human locals, where, for a while, they share the work and the peace of mind. "Until one day" a shiny object is recovered from a rice paddy and all hell breaks loose. The bottle cap, of course. That's all it takes. Before long, they've spotted others capping Scrooge's remaining bottles and that's it. They're after him. Anything for a bottle cap—two hundred pigs, a brick factory. To restore the equilibrium, Scrooge sends Donald over the mountains to arrange for a series of airdrops. For a moment it seems to work as economics takes effect, reducing the bottle cap to something like the German mark of 1923. But it's too much. The planes keep coming. Donald, parachuting in, beams to announce the rest of the airlift on its way—one plane an hour every day for the next six weeks. They head for the hills. It's raining bottle caps. The paddies start to choke. The pastures fill. He might as well have never come. It's just the same. How strange, the shovels and the baskets filled like money buckets. "Don't you know it's useless, Uncle Scrooge?" we want to cry although we love it and we know that's not the point.

ALWAYS SHALL HAVE BEEN

———

I
T'S ME AND BOBBY SPEARS AND SOME OTHER KID, A FRIEND OF
Bobby's, and we're armed, after a fashion, and making an in-
cursion into the somewhat hilly, lightly forested, strangely
empty realm along the ravine that runs behind the Cotton
Bowling Palace, south below some old pink brick apartments
and eventually into a park, a sort of park, behind our school,
Rusk Junior High. Another year and we're too old for this. It's
our last chance, in a way, though we don't think of it like that.
We do not think. Last chance for what? I'm not quite sure.
We're armed with two- or two-and-a-half-foot two-by-fours,
each fitted out with a pair of heavy rubber bands secured with
staples or nails at the front end, then drawn back as far as you
dared into the jaws of wooden clothespins wired to the board—
new clothespins, preferably, bright of wood and stiff of spring.
A flat, round pebble slipped into each rubber band ahead of the
clothespin and you've got a double-shooter. Put your eye out.
Break a window. Send some kid home with his hand up to his
head. You didn't mean it, but you did. The clear and terrible
ambivalence of power.

How did we come to agree that this was a good idea? Were

other thoughts put forward? No? Apparently not. Okay. So I'll
be here with the weapons in the morning. Saturday morning.
Gray and empty. Was the bowling alley open yet? Perhaps. I
think it opened pretty early. There were these huge translu-
cent, variously colored hemispheres around it in a zigzag, up
and down, so when sequentially illuminated it was like a colorful stream of giant bouncing balls. Of bouncing bowling balls I
guess, although that's not a thing you ever want to see. It was
spectacular at night. But in the grayness of the morning, kind
of strange. We passed beneath the bouncing balls into a parking lot in the back, past storage structures, then just grass and
weeds that sloped down to the ravine, where we spread out the
way you do when making an incursion and proceeded to the
south, encountering no one. This is history. This is deep, recoverable narrative. Even though we're only children. Barely children still. We'd managed to arrive at certain actions, certain
attitudes relating to a place that made it history. We are breathless. Were a journal left behind, the final words would be "proceeding to the south, encountering no one."

What has happened here—in the silliest and most literal
way—is the capture of a moment. Of a place within the moment. What exhilarates—and I believe we were exhilarated,
rubber-band guns all directed down the dark arcade of trees
along the stream—was how we found ourselves within this
empty space that seemed, by force of arms, "available" (as
Nancy says), divested, inexplicably, of all associations; opened
up, a gash of unwrapped, unhealed territory bare to these
events, to be impressed by them forever. That's like history, I
should think. What makes it different from our ordinary lives.
The moment felt—not as event but just as moment—to the
point of anguish. Maybe one has heard about such things. Real
war, real soldiers come upon a sort of pause, a sort of gap that's

been torn open and there's nothing they can say or do. Just stand there as if such events had no place else to go, no place to be except the here and now. That's history, I imagine. What a thing, to come upon it here like this. Slight, smiley, freckled Bobby Spears just up the slope, his nameless friend across the stream, against a tree. They take on sweet and fragile qualities. From where I stand. The cost of immortality, I guess, is this fragility. This sweetness, strangely, like the feeling you get from certain Mathew Brady photographs—as if that bloody ground were never here before this moment, that this moment, which requires a kind of violence to establish or discover, stands for all. It is a matter of intention. We intend to take this ground as we intend to live forever. Always shall have been intending.

At some point we let it go. Fire off our rounds into the shadowy air downstream. These silly weapons are not accurate— your pebble slips off center, shoots off sideways. Half the time, though, it goes sort of where intended, most satisfactorily with a definite spin imparted to the pebble, which recedes with this extraordinary zinging sound as if it had been shot along an actual thread extending from your eye into the distance. We split up and head back home. And then it's noon and time for lunch. We live forever. Always shall have lived forever.

STILL-LIFE PAINTING

—

I AM CLEANING OUT THE STORAGE SPACE THAT'S UNDER THE
stairs but accessed from outside—a steel door somewhat
strangely opening onto the grass. Twenty years of stuff di-
verted here. Not quite tossed out. You never know. I hate to see
it in a way, to drag the splitting cardboard boxes into the sun
and pull them open—not so much, I think, for the sad associations as the sadness of the things themselves, that sense of deep
removal that comes over things as soon, almost as soon, as they
leave your hand. The kinds of things that come and go, that
seem to circulate right through as if obedient to a metabolic
process—here it's knickknacks, souvenir-type things, all kinds
of thoughtless objects, plastic toys, and small stuffed animals.
The fundamental stuff that, scattered, say, along the path of a
tornado, looks like blood.

And then, oh my, among the scatter, what is here? A little
painting in the sunlight. One of my mom's—an early still life,
signed and dated. I have a stack of later efforts; nothing's ever
signed or dated. Flora Searcy 63. Perhaps she liked this one. I
like it. Very simple. Much more studious than later ones. On
cheap, warped canvas panel. I think maybe I remember it: her

painting it, that big white stoneware pitcher, next to which she's placed a pear and a carnation—d'Anjou pear and red carnation. All around me in the grass there's all this stuff, tornadic debris or maybe parts of something awaiting reassembly, and I'm standing with this little still-life painting like instructions— how to have such things, regard them in a calm, considered manner. Pitcher, pear, and red carnation. But, of course, it could be anything. Take any of these objects, dust them off, and set them up and paint their picture. From disorder, out of darkness, comes this quiet, measured longing. Things brought close enough to paint are within reach. Within that critical range where they present themselves as things to have, to be desired. You think this sort of thing is mostly just for practice. Things stay put. The light is constant. It will wait for you one Sunday to the next. But it is always more than that. Look how she reaches for the roundness of the bottom of the pitcher like a sightless person. Feeling with her brush the white go gray, then umber. Little arc of white—impasto, gestural, cautiously gestural—where the base splays out to catch the light again. And these things placed against, upon these practically uninflected surfaces. I love that. Nothing interferes —just horizontal bands of different grays to make a table or a ledge. And then behind, an indeterminate dark gray distance. Everything's a little hazy, glimpsed through gauze. Desire has flattened, saddened, paled. The best my mom could do. But not so bad, I think. The pallid gauziness itself a kind of touching, or longing to be touching; an admission—an unconscious one; it happens on its own—but an admission as to distance, loss, regret, perhaps. A little. Things recede from us. She knows that—always knew it from her childhood. She must know that in this place where things get blown about and tossed away, there's something in the temporary weight of that carnation. She has caught the gentle crush of it. The frailest object here conveys the weight, conducts the mass and heft of longing—faint, impermanent as fragrance—into the picture.

Did you know that in the thousand years or so between antiquity and the Renaissance there was no still-life painting in the West? Can you imagine? A thousand years. No pictures of nonsubservient things by themselves. Through all that time such things are lost to us as self-sufficient facts. Those things the ancients loved to depict as if to touch, as if to have as they adorned their private houses with mosaics and painted pictures of the sorts of party favors, food, and trinkets given to guests. *Look what there is for you,* the pictures from Pompeii and Herculaneum seem to say, *Look what there is to have, for a while at least, here in this dangerous world.* One's thoughts are poised above these things—the fish, the pomegranates, writing implements, little piles of coins—like one of those coin-operated mechanical claws above the tray of prizes. Yet all that is taken away. Things by themselves fall out of favor. For a thousand years or so those simple objects of experience that happen to appear in sacred pictures (on and on, the sacred pictures) have been cleansed of mundane qualities. Removed from us and placed in higher service. You can't have them. Can't even desire them, really. For to do so was a moral and a philosophical error. Mundane objects in themselves had slipped beyond our contemplation. Theologically, philosophically, things by themselves fell into doubt. The particular world was an unintelligible emanation from the mind of God. Things merely in themselves, Saint Augustine tells us (and Aquinas too, though later, more forgiving of the body), are not understood directly. Our minds cannot seize the object, cannot fully know the thing itself. How poor and cold to have it settle out like that, as I suppose it must have done to some extent, into the ordinary life. To have one's love glance off the object of desire. To lose acquaintance, in some fundamental way, with grapes and lemons and dead rabbits. I remember reading *Robin Hood*—the Junior Deluxe edition so beautifully written and illustrated by Howard Pyle—and receiving such a powerful and physical impression of medieval life that I carry it with me still. But that's not it. That can't be how it really was. So clear, meticulous, and carefully observed. Each tree with roots. Each pie and goblet on each table drawn to reveal itself as just its worldly qualities within the worldly moment:

> So the ale was brought and given to Little John. Then, blowing the froth a little away to make room for his lips, he tilted the bottom of the pot higher and higher, till it pointed to the sky, and he had to shut his eyes to keep the dazzle of the sunshine out of them. Then he took the pot away, for there was nothing in it, and heaved a full deep sigh, looking at the others with moist eyes and shaking his head solemnly.

In fact, Little John would never have achieved, in the late twelfth century, where this version places him, quite so bright and deep an understanding of his pot of ale in the sunlight. That would surely have required a firmer grasp of the things at hand, of the actuality of sensible experience, than was available two hundred years or so before the particular world began to spring from under snowy generalities. Little John as here portrayed—brought, as it were, out of the dark—is given a nominalist pot of ale. An anti-Platonic pot of ale whose self-sufficiency reflects his own as he shakes his head not just from the satisfaction of having had his ale but also from his having *comprehended* it. And that's really the thing: the comprehension of the sensible world. That it took a thousand years to return to our senses. For the plausible, comprehensible bits of everyday life to begin to poke through here and there like crocuses at last into the wintry holy images. At first a certain pregnant specificity. And then all hell breaks loose. Abundance now becomes depictable with a clearly ravenous accuracy and heedlessness of seasonal propriety. And about this time as well, you start to see, detached from reverential duty, portraits. Independent pictures of us gazing from and out into the ordinary world. And which, in the case of Arcimboldo—those bizarre "composite heads" constructed entirely of game and fruits and various edibles representing, surely, the fullest comprehension of the sensible world—disclose that we can truly *be* all this and eat it, too. We are profoundly what we eat. What we desire. We love this stuff. And by extension, stuff in general. All the other real and suddenly depictable things. The pots and pans and fancy knobbed Venetian glassware. At some level everything aspires, accedes, to the condition of the edible. As an infant understands. We're infantile before all this. It's like we've never really seen all this before. Or had forgotten. It becomes a little crazy. Like the repeal of Prohibition. Though constrained to carry certain admonitions—a biblical scene, say, or a statue of Martin Luther in the background.

Here's a picture by Pieter Aertsen dated 1552. It's as sublime a picture of meat as you could want. It brings the longing and the guilt into unbearable—somehow lurid, somehow touching—opposition. In the foreground is a jumble of all manner of desirable stuff that would have come to hand and mouth, albeit wealthy hand and mouth, in the sixteenth century. Wonderful stuff. You think, Oh my, that's what they had. It's so detailed. You're so convinced. It's not just that they had that sort of thing—that sort of pewter flagon, biscuit, money bag, key, lock, pot, pot of flowers. They had *these*. These ones right here. And hovering over all, they had this joint of meat. This massive, luminous leg of mutton, pork, or whatever glowing softly at the center of the painting in a golden light that feels like afternoon. You glimpse the apology, the guilt, way in the background. Through a portal you can see, rather stiffly and sketchily rendered, a scene from the Gospel of Luke: Christ in the house of Mary and Martha. It's overwhelmed by the joint of meat, which seems to pose before it as before some nineteenth-century photographer's decorative screen—very much, in fact, like one of those ample Victorian nudes on a naughty postcard displaying herself in front of some bit of classical scenery to exonerate somewhat the prurient gaze.

Then by the century's end, it's just too much—all this confronted guilt and longing. It collapses into the first pure still-life paintings since antiquity—the admonition now implicit in the wilting leaf, the wormhole in the apple. Most spectacularly, though, in the still-life pictures of Juan Sánchez Cotán, it clarifies into the purest possible terms. It's one of those moments when the first glimpse of a thing, of an idea, remains the best. The guilt goes black. Imponderable dark, imponderable space in front of which our desire, ungoverned, undiffused by homely context, goes straight at, attaches to, becomes almost a property of the simple vegetables, fruits, and game birds placed or suspended, Joseph Cornell–like, within the perfectly squared and smooth and, one imagines, cold stone window. And they're all like this. These simple still-life paintings. They are all this cold stone window—opening onto empty space or the uninflected dark of the previous thousand years or original sin or that regret I sense in my mother's little painting vastly concentrated, purified to black—in which, in brilliant raking light, we see the things we love, the exact particular things we love exactly, perfectly, self-sufficiently painted and arranged against the abyss as if to say, All right, you can have these things but you have to come to the window.

And that light, the raking light, somehow surprises. Like a door has been opened somewhere accidentally. Oh, we're sorry. We thought this was the door to sumptuous floral arrangements, table settings, stuff like that—not this control room or whatever it is. Prop storage. Not the place where our desire is kept forever in its blazing perishability in the dark.

There aren't that many. Only one dated—1602. And probably all about that time. In 1603 Sánchez Cotán took holy orders. So would I, I have to think. Having summed it up as best I could. With nothing more to say about it. That might seem like a pretty good plan. Or maybe simply pack it up with little notes on the cardboard boxes. Shove it all back into the dark. Except the painting, I suppose. Hang on to that. But shove the rest back into the dark where it belongs.

TELL THE WORLD THIS BOOK WAS

GOOD	BAD	SO-SO

ACKNOWLEDGMENTS

M Y GRATITUDE FIRST AND ALWAYS TO NANCY REBAL, GUIDING angel, for knowing what it means.

To Ben Fountain, relentlessly generous friend and neighbor, for getting it out there.

To J. J. Sullivan, Lorin Stein, and John Freeman for encouragements, connections, and publication.

To my editor, Andy Ward, and my agent, Nicole Aragi, for ganging up to show me the book I needed to write—for her enthusiasm and wisdom, and his dowsing-rod intelligence that knows exactly where, without disturbing the ground, to pause, to dig.

To my old friend and scientific adviser, Charles Alonzo Watson III.

To Lila King Schroeder, who told the first story.

To Greear Cossitt, for the words that made the title.

To Bonnie Thompson, for her sensitive and meticulous copyediting.

To my kids, John, Elizabeth, and Anna, and their mother, Jean.

And to friends and informants living and dead: Steve Anderson, Professor Annemarie Weyl Carr, Professor John Cotton, Tim and Melanie Coursey, Dogan the driver, Charlie Drum, Mike and Anita Edgmon, Dave England, John Fountain, Vernon Grissom, Luke Heister, Tracy Hicks, Kyle Hobratschk, Reverend Dr. John C. Holbert, Courtney and Elaine King, Paul Larson, Alan Lidji, Fay Lidji, Professor John Lunsford, Doug MacWithey, Kevin MacWithey, Daniel McKenna, Charles Dee Mitchell, Ufuk Ozsoy, Jack Powell, Steve Richardson, Bobo Riefler, Babbette Samuels, Alpay Burak Seven, Ron Siebler, Bobby Spears, Neil Sreenan, Bob Trammell, Karan Verma, Professor Mary Vernon, Nolan White, Bryan Woolley, and Alp Yaradanakul.

ABOUT THE AUTHOR

DAVID SEARCY is the author of *Ordinary Horror*
and *Last Things,* and the recipient of a grant by
the National Endowment for the Arts. He lives
in Dallas, Texas.

This book was set in Dante, a typeface designed by Giovanni Mardersteig (1892–1977). Conceived as a private type for the Officina Bodoni in Verona, Italy, Dante was originally cut only for hand composition by Charles Malin, the famous Parisian punch cutter, between 1946 and 1952. Its first use was in an edition of Boccaccio's *Trat tatello in laude di Dante* that appeared in 1954. The Monotype Corporation's version of Dante followed in 1957. Though modeled on the Aldine type used for Pietro Cardinal Bembo's treatise *De Aetna* in 1495, Dante is a thoroughly modern interpretation of that venerable face.